AN EARLY HISTORY
of the
WYOMING VALLEY

D1608181

An Early History
of the
Wyoming Valley

The Yankee-Pennamite Wars & Timothy Pickering

Kathleen A. Earle, PhD

THE
History
PRESS

Published by The History Press
Charleston, SC
www.historypress.com

Cover images courtesy of Stephen B. Killian, Esquire, Wilkes-Barre, Pennsylvania.

First published 2022

Manufactured in the United States

ISBN 9781467149594

Library of Congress Control Number: 2021952401

Notice: The information in this book is true and complete to the best of our knowledge. It is offered without guarantee on the part of the author or The History Press. The author and The History Press disclaim all liability in connection with the use of this book.

To my wise and wonderful children, Seann, Thomas and Susie:
Honor your ancestors, but learn from their mistakes.

CONTENTS

PREFACE AND
ACKNOWLEDGMENTS

The story of the Yankee-Pennamite wars in Pennsylvania has received scant attention from historians. This conflict occurred largely between 1769 and 1790, and its history is confounded by the occurrence of the American Revolution and the founding of the United States of America during the same time frame. This interplay is further complicated by the presence and active participation of the powerful Haudenosaunee, or Iroquois, tribe in colonial historical events, a role not usually featured in narratives of the time.

The Yankee-Pennamite wars were fought over ownership of a piece of land that had been granted twice, once to William Penn and once to the Colony of Connecticut, by King Charles II of England. Both the Connecticut Yankees and the Pennsylvania Pennamites fought fiercely for what they believed was theirs.

The kidnapping of Timothy Pickering in 1788 is a footnote in this little-known war. Yet the capture of this Pennsylvania official by a band of fifteen young rascals largely brought the conflict to an end.

This book would not have been written without Paula Radwanski of the Wyoming County Historical Society (WCHS) in Tunkhannock, Pennsylvania. When I contacted her in March 2016 looking for information about persons by the name of "Earl" in the Wyoming Valley, Paula told me about the kidnapping of Timothy Pickering by, among others, the three Earl boys. For the previous three decades, I had been searching for the father of my ancestor John Earl, born in 1795 in Geneva, New York. This new information led to several years of research in Tunkhannock and environs, looking for the link of these three young men to my ancestor. I found nothing definitive, but there are tantalizing clues.

What I did find was that the story of the Yankee-Pennamite wars and the events during this time in the Wyoming Valley made a fascinating tale that needed to be told. And so I have, as much as my ability as a social scientist, rather than a historian, has allowed.

I had help along the way, beginning with my neighbor in Maine, Jane Merrill, who suggested that I write down the story that was absorbing my attention and time. I was encouraged through several fits and starts by Michael McGandy, senior editor at Cornell University Press. I am extremely grateful to editor J. Banks Smither of The History Press, who has cheerfully and enthusiastically guided me through the process of producing this book.

Paula Radwanski and her colleague Sherry Shiffer of WCHS have continued to provide comments and guidance. I also received valuable feedback and access to historic illustrations from the Luzerne County Historical Society (LCHS) in Wilkes-Barre, Pennsylvania. Amanda Fontenova, director of library and archives, has provided an illuminating discussion of the differences in historical perspective regarding the Battle of Wyoming. Other LCHS members who assisted in the creation of this book are Mary Walsh, interim executive director, and Mark Riccetti Jr., director of operations and programs. They led me to Stephen Killian, Esquire, who commented on an early version of the manuscript and who provided a colorful and engaging tour of the site of the Battle of Wyoming on a cold March morning in 2021. Steve also graciously permitted me to use some of the Wyoming Valley illustrations that he has collected over the years.

I am grateful to my friend Merrilee Goldsmith Brown for an early edit of the book and to my husband, Stan Fox, who has provided advice and ongoing support. He has also been my companion, driver and photographer for many of the trips I took to the Wyoming Valley and upstate New York in pursuit of information regarding the Wyoming Valley and the kidnappers of Timothy Pickering.

INTRODUCTION

O
n June 26, 1788, fifteen young men kidnapped Colonel Timothy Pickering, notable Pennsylvania official, from his home in Wilkes-Barre, Pennsylvania. The young men were backcountry woodsmen and farmers who wore blackface and stuck feathers in their hair during the abduction. They carried guns, hatchets and knives, although they later said they brought them only to scare the colonel, not to hurt him.

The kidnappers were almost all descendants of the first wave of immigrants to the American colonies between the landing of the Mayflower in 1620 and the English civil war in 1640. Their forebears had been proud officeholders, elected officials in their towns and churches, men who fought in the French and Indian War and the American Revolution. By the earliest years of the United States of America, in the northeastern corner of Pennsylvania known as the Wyoming Valley, they and their families had come upon hard times. This was largely due to the misguided generosity of King Charles II of England and the tortuous events that resulted.

In the mid-seventeenth century, King Charles, unaware of the geography of the land in question, had inadvertently given the top third of what is now Pennsylvania to both the Connecticut Colony and to William Penn. To complicate matters further, the land was already under the jurisdiction of the Haudenosaunee, who were allowing the Delaware tribe to live there. The fierce Haudenosaunee, or Iroquois, had subjugated many of the other tribes in their extensive territory, which ranged from southern Ontario, Canada, to the Susquehanna region of Pennsylvania and from the

Adirondack Mountains to Lake Erie in New York. The Six Nations of the Iroquois Confederacy include the Mohawk, Oneida, Onondaga, Cayuga, Seneca and Tuscarora.

When the Connecticut people began to survey their new land along the rich bottomland of the mighty Susquehanna River in 1753, members of the Haudenosaunee and the Pennsylvanians were alarmed. Thus began a war between the Wild Yankees and the Pennamites that would last for four decades. During that time, the American Revolution came and went, and General John Sullivan marched with 2,500 men from Pennsylvania to Canada on a mission to destroy the Iroquois Confederacy.

The Haudenosaunee played a major role in the events that transpired in and around the Wyoming Valley. A proud and powerful people, their fate was sealed by fighting alongside the British and Tories in the American Revolution, leading to Sullivan's march.

There were two Wyoming massacres. The first was in 1763, reputedly by the Delaware. The second was in 1778, during the Revolution, by a large force of British, Tory and Haudenosaunee that easily overwhelmed the few Connecticut families in the valley. Rumors quickly spread about the horrific acts perpetrated during the second massacre, and in retribution, in 1779, Sullivan's soldiers marched from the Wyoming Valley to northwestern New York, burning Iroquois villages and orchards, killing livestock and destroying extensive fields of corn and other crops. They lost several cows off the steep cliffs between Tunkhannock and Queen Esther's Castle, scalped an occasional Haudenosaunee brave and shot fifty exhausted pack horses, whose heads were later arranged along the road to the since-named town of Horseheads. The Haudenosaunee, seeing their warriors were outnumbered, mostly fled, leaving their empty houses, their orchards, gardens and livestock to be raided and destroyed.

And the Yankees and the Pennamites battled on. Both sides took to dressing like Natives, smearing on blackface and putting feathers in their hair, whooping and hollering as they attacked each other.

Their decades-long war came to a head when Pickering arrived in Wilkes-Barre in 1787 to broker a solution to the competing land claims. One of his first actions was to jail the popular leader of the Yankees, John Franklin. A captain in the Revolution and a volunteer on Sullivan's march, Franklin was an early settler in the valley, a justice of the peace and a generous man, who married the widow of a man killed in the second Wyoming massacre and raised her several children.

When he was jailed, word got back that he was cold and hungry, uncared for in a bare cell. The Connecticut settlers came up with a plan to free him: a group of hardy young Yankees would capture Pickering and hold him in the woods until the authorities agreed to free Franklin. Fifteen young men, referred to from then on as "the Boys," were promised land and money for "a frolic" if they would do the deed.

The Boys kept Pickering, well fed and cared for, in the woods for almost three weeks. He asked for and received by courier a pound of chocolate, a quill and paper, gloves, a copy of the latest sermons preached in his church. One of the Boys carried him on his back from the boat to the riverbank so his feet would not get wet. They gave him the best cut of a fawn they had killed in the woods. They gave him tips about farming and livestock.

On July 15, 1788, nineteen days after they had kidnapped him, with Franklin still in jail, the Boys let him go.

Chapter 1

THE KIDNAPPING

On a steamy June night in the year 1788, Timothy Pickering was standing in his bedroom in Wilkes-Barre, Pennsylvania, his feverish nine-month-old son in his arms. Suddenly the door was pushed open, and someone shouted, "Get up." Rebecca Pickering jumped out of bed, threw on a robe and ran to the kitchen to get a candle. When she returned, she and Timothy saw in the dim candlelight several young, black-faced men with feathers stuck in their hair. Some had handkerchiefs tied around their heads. They flourished knives, guns and tomahawks. These were Wild Yankees, young white men who stormed out of the tangled hills along the Susquehanna River to attack their Pennsylvania neighbors.

In Pickering's own words:

> *Their first act was to pinion me; tying my arms together, with a cord, above my elbows, and crossed over my back. To the middle of this cord they tied another, long enough for one of them to take hold of, to prevent my escaping from them.*[1]

Pickering angrily demanded to know who had accosted the sanctity of his Wilkes-Barre home. He was, after all, an important man. Born in Salem, Massachusetts, in 1745, Pickering graduated from Harvard in 1763, was admitted to the Massachusetts bar, held several offices in Salem, entered

Timothy Pickering House, 130 South Main Street, Wilkes-Barre, Luzerne County, PA. Built 1786 and demolished 1931. *Stanley Jones, photographer; Historic American Buildings Survey (HABS), US government.*

the American Revolution as a colonel and was appointed adjutant general by George Washington. He became quartermaster of the army in 1780. In 1787 Pickering was sent to settle conflicting land claims and establish order in northeastern Pennsylvania.

For three decades there had been a difference of opinion stewing in the Wyoming Valley between two factions that each believed they had a right to the warm bottomland of the Susquehanna River. The Connecticut Colony and William Penn had both been granted the same piece of land by Charles II of Great Britain, in 1662 and 1681, respectively. The two sides were defined as "New England" and "Pennsylvania" by William Judd, who tried in early 1787 to warn his fellow Connecticut settlers about the fairness of sending Pickering to resolve these jurisdictional claims:

> *I thought it my duty solemnly to warn you to be cautious and not to leap before you look and clearly see your way lest you repent your folly when too late....Col. Pickering is an artful man and made use of (being of New England extract) to deceive you—he is interested under Pennsylvania—beware of this disguise.*[2]

One of the first things Pickering did was jail the Connecticut leader, John Franklin. In October 1787 Franklin was placed in a cold and miserable Philadelphia jail cell, where he was given insufficient food and only allowed to wear the light suit he had on when captured. As Franklin's health and spirit failed, leaders of the Connecticut faction planned to kidnap Timothy Pickering in order to exchange him for their leader.

On June 26 the kidnappers, whom Pickering referred to as "ruffians," told him to bring a blanket or outer coat, as he would be away for some time. With a "surtout" over his arm, Pickering was led by a rope through the sleeping village of Wilkes-Barre, flanked by Boys on every side. Pickering counted fifteen. After a walk of several miles up the Susquehanna River, they stopped at a Pittstown tavern for some whiskey. The Boys offered whiskey to their captive, but, bragged Pickering, "I did not accept; I drank water." While continuing quietly through the silent town, one of his captors said to Pickering, "Now if you will only write two or three lines to the Executive Council, they will discharge Colonel Franklin, and then we will release you." Pickering replied haughtily, "The Executive Council better understand their duty, than to discharge a traitor to procure the release of an innocent man." "Damn him, why don't you tomahawk him?" was the response regarding Pickering from the ranks.[3]

The kidnappers and their associates were young and brash; most were in their twenties and the youngest, a courier for the kidnappers, only fifteen.[4] Because they painted their faces black, they were originally called "the Black Boys," eventually just "the Boys."

Continuing on their midnight journey, Pickering and his captors reached a canoe on the Lackawanna River and took turns crossing in the dark. When it came to Pickering's turn, he wrote in his diary, one of the boys "waded to the shore—laid down his pack—returned to the side of the canoe, *and carried me on his back to the shore.*"[5]

At one point they saw a man leading a horse on the other side of the river, and one of the captors cried out, "There goes Major Jenkins now, a damned stinking son of a bitch."[6] It was apparently one of the Connecticut leaders, John Jenkins, who was now on his way to the Lakes, a reference to the Finger Lakes of New York. The Boys assumed he was turning tail, deserting the undertaking that he and his colleagues had conceived.

John Jenkins and his brother Stephen had promised the Boys land and money "to make a frolic" if they would capture Pickering. They said prominent figures in the land dispute would support them by marching to Philadelphia with five hundred men.

The kidnapping party continued to the Susquehanna River and crossed on a scow, eventually arriving at a log home owned by the family of kidnapper Timothy Kilborn. There they stopped to rest and to eat.

The boys carried Pickering from the boat so his feet would not get wet. *Original painting by Kathleen A. Earle.*

Throughout his captivity, Pickering shared the food of his captors; in one case he was given the prime cut of a fawn. Pickering wrote in his journal:

> *A fire being quickly kindled, they began to cook some of the venison. The hunter took his first cut. They sharpened small sticks at both ends, running one into a slice of the fawn and setting the other end into the ground, the top of the stick bearing so near the fire as to broil the flesh. Being hungry, I borrowed one of their knives, and followed their example.—I observed the hunter tending his steak with great nicety; and sprinkling it with a little salt, as soon as it was done, he with a very good grace, presented it to me!*[7]

Occasionally the food was not to his taste:

> *At first, they had some good salt pork, and wheaten bread that lasted two or three days, after which they got Indian meal, which they made into cakes, or fried, as pancakes, in the fat of the pork. Of the pork they were very sparing; frying only two or three small slices at a time and cutting them up in the pan. Such was our breakfast, dinner, and supper: my share did not exceed*

five mouthfuls of pork at each meal. They fared better—sopping up, with their bread or cakes, all the fat in the pan, of which I felt no inclination to participate—It was here I told them they would repent of their doings; and instead of being supported by four hundred men in the county, as they had professed to believe, that they would be abandoned to their fate.[8]

When they reached the woods, the Boys took turns guarding their captive and running off to get news or supplies from sympathetic supporters. Captive and captors slept in the open, but when a thunderstorm wet them to the bone, they retreated to a nearby log cottage and dried their clothes. They moved frequently to avoid detection by the local sheriff and Pennsylvania militia. On July 3 there were shots fired across the river, and the next day the militia attacked the kidnappers with twelve or fourteen men. One Boy was shot in the hand, and the leader of the attackers was wounded in this encounter.

Despite occasional skirmishes and lack of supplies, Pickering's captivity was mostly benign. From July 3 to 10 he wrote in his journal:

Wrote to my wife for camlet coat, 2 pairs worsted hose, 1 shirt, 1 pocket handkerchief, 1 towel, needle; thread, yarn, leather gloves, 4 yards yellow binding, a bag [1 lb. chocolate], ½ lb. soap, [1 lb. sugar], ½ quire paper, shoes, 2 quills, penknife, Dr. Price's Sermons, fine comb.

A log cabin in the Wyoming Valley around 1788. *In Munsell,* History of Luzerne, Lackawanna and Wyoming Counties, PA, *1880.*

19

> *Sent a large wooden spoon & butter spoon to Kilburn's, to be sent thence to my wife.*
>
> *Gave Woodward a letter dated yesterday to forward to my wife. Desired her to send me a small tin kettle with a cover. Woodward returned—says my things are at Marcy's with a letter for me.*[9]

He also wrote in his journal that David Woodward instructed him in how to care for sows after they give birth, how to plow corn with oxen so the corn is not damaged and when to breed heifers. He received other advice as well, such as how to identify edible bark and berries and make coffee from toasted wheat bread. "'Tis a very tolerable drink," reported Pickering.

Pickering stated that Gideon Dudley wanted to manacle him in handcuffs near the beginning of the ordeal; however, Pickering wrote in his journal:

> *Mr. Earl (whom I had not known, but who was father to two of the party) interposed—telling Dudley that there was no danger of an escape, and advising him not to put the irons on me. He accordingly forbore.*[10]

Joseph Earl was one of the elderly men from Tunkhannock, and he was related to the three Earl boys, Daniel, Solomon and Benjamin, who were among the fifteen kidnappers. Daniel Earl later stated they had met right before the kidnapping on a hill behind Joseph Earl's house. Joseph testified on July 19 that he was not at home at the time, and when he returned home his wife was crying and told him that the Boys had gone to take Colonel Pickering. Joseph stated that the Boys brought the colonel to his house to eat at least three times and that at one point he was tied with a rope, and Joseph released him.

Later Pickering was chained by the ankle to a tree by Daniel Taylor and Timothy Kilborn. This was on the orders of the stated leader of the kidnappers, John Hyde, because, according to Pickering:

> *Col. Franklin, they said, had been put in irons, in the Philadelphia jail, and they must put irons on me, although it was not agreeable to them to do it; "but their great men required it."…This chain, besides its conformity with the orders of their "great men," saved my gentlemen from the burden of mounting guard every night.*[11]

The chain was attached to the leg of one of the captors while he slept, so that he would wake up if Pickering tried to escape. The colonel did not object, figuring the Boys would soon get tired of their misguided plan to trade him for Franklin and would let him go.

On July 19, 1788, Timothy Pickering wrote a letter to Benjamin Franklin:

> *I have the pleasure to inform you and the honorable Council that I am restored to my liberty. The band of ruffians who took me, finding themselves unsupported, even by the men who advised and directed them in the affair, came to me last Monday with proposals to set me at liberty, saying they had been advisd by their friends & one of the magistrates whom they had seen, to make their peace with me, & petition Council for a pardon.*[12]

Later, charges were filed against the kidnappers, their *great men* and their relatives and associates. Some of the Boys were jailed, some were fined and several of the accused fled to the Finger Lakes area of New York.

Chapter 2

BACKGROUND

The genesis of the kidnapping of Timothy Pickering occurred more than a century earlier. During the 1660s, while North American settlers were defining the boundaries of their newly founded colonies, the kings of Europe were distracted by difficulties at home.

In 1661, King Charles II (1630–85) had just returned to power in England after a nine-year rule by Oliver Cromwell. Cromwell had overthrown Charles I in the first English Civil War, causing Charles II to relocate to France.

When Charles II returned to Britain after the death of Cromwell, it is rumored, he commissioned a statue of himself on a horse with Oliver Cromwell underfoot.

Upon his return from France, King Charles began to take an interest in his British holdings abroad. This was noted by the colonists. Concerned that the king would attempt to take control of the colonies, the governor of the Connecticut Colony, John Winthrop Jr., sailed to England in 1661 and returned with the Charter of 1662, which granted the colony "all that part of New England…bounded on the east by the Narragansett Bay… and…from the said Narragansett Bay on the East, to the South Sea on the West Part."[13]

Northern and southern boundaries were to remain the same, with the colony extending westward to the South Sea, now called the Pacific Ocean. The South Sea (Pacific Ocean) was well known to navigators, but its exact location was apparently unclear to the Connecticut Colony—and

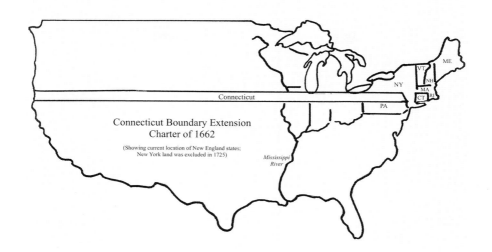

Map of the Connecticut Colony in 1662, as described by King Charles II, from sea to sea. *Drawing by Kathleen A. Earle.*

to King Charles II. A later agreement with the colony of New York in 1725 excluded that portion of the newly refigured colony of Connecticut encompassing the southern tip of New York State.

In addition to granting Connecticut a huge swath of the land from the Atlantic to the Pacific, provisions of the Charter of 1662 gave the governor and freemen of Connecticut a clear legal basis for their colony, a generous degree of self-government and freedom to lease, grant, sell, bargain and dispose of their property.

About twenty years later, in 1681, King Charles II deeded land to William Penn (1644–1718) to settle the king's debt of £16,000 to Penn's father, Admiral Sir William Penn. The Charter of Pennsylvania, named after Admiral Penn, assured the colony the protection of England. In 1682 William Penn laid out a Quaker settlement, and by 1685 he had sold six hundred shares, covering seven hundred thousand acres. Besides English Quakers, investors from Germany, Holland, France, Scotland and Ireland purchased shares, and many of them settled the land between the time of its purchase and the American Revolution.

Unfortunately, the grant by King Charles to William Penn included some of the property deeded to Connecticut, consisting of approximately the northeastern third of what is now Pennsylvania.

No one really paid much attention to the misguided and redundant generosity of King Charles, transportation and means of communication being difficult. Not until, that is, the middle of the eighteenth century, when residents of eastern Connecticut began to run out of land to divide among their sons.

On March 29, 1753, ninety-two inhabitants of Windham County in Connecticut requested land from the Connecticut legislature upon the Susquehanna River at a place called Quimanuk, which was later called Wyoming, designating a valley eighteen miles long and from three to five miles wide.[14] The Connecticut Assembly rejected the request.

A few months later, in July of 1753, the Susquehannah Company of Hartford, Connecticut, was formed to realize Connecticut's claim. In 1754, the Susquehannah Company paid £2,000 to fourteen Haudenosaunee chiefs for the land that had been deeded by King Charles. At the same meeting, Pennsylvania purchased land in southwestern Pennsylvania for £400.[15] According to George E. McCracken (1979), the Pennsylvanians told the Haudenosaunee that they could continue to use the Wyoming Valley land as hunting grounds and that no Whites would move there.

Armed with King Charles's decree, the Company began to sell shares of land in the Wyoming Valley. Speculators quickly bought into the plan, initially for two dollars a share. The response was overwhelming, so that by November 1754 there were eight hundred subscribers and the entrance fee had gone up to nine dollars per share.

A party of surveyors under John Jenkins Sr. went to the valley in 1753. Due to the presence of several hostile groups of Natives, they shortly returned home, where a map was created showing the location of the tribal villages and places of rendezvous.

The Wyoming Valley was at that time inhabited primarily by the Delaware tribe. They were under the protection of the League of the Iroquois, or Haudenosaunee.

In 1755 the Delaware Company was formed in Connecticut to oversee purchase of land between the Susquehannah Company's purchase and the Delaware River. They paid the Delaware tribe 500 milled dollars and English goods. The leader of the Delaware, Teedyuscung, was an impressive man who had tangled with the Iroquois and was spokesman for his people with the Whites; he was described as lusty, raw-boned, haughty and desirous of respect. The bearing and appearance of this "King of the Delaware" is important to note, as the Haudenosaunee were opposed to any such haughty displays of dominance by their own leaders.

Indian Massacre at Wilkesbarre (Valley of Wyoming). John Rogers, engraver; F.O.C. Darley, artist. 1878. *Collection of Stephen B. Killian, Esq., Wilkes-Barre, Pennsylvania.*

The Delaware occupied the town of Wyalusing, above the site of modern Wilkes-Barre. Moravian missionaries, with the permission of the Haudenosaunee, had converted the Delaware to Christianity. European-style civilization began to take hold. Lands were fenced, and horses, hens and cows were raised. A school was built, as well as a chapel with a bell that sounded across the Susquehanna River valley.

From 1754 to 1762 the Connecticut Yankees petitioned both the English king and the Connecticut legislature to send a group of settlers to the Wyoming Valley, but they did not receive a reply. This was during the French and Indian War, and perhaps their attention was elsewhere. Finally, in the spring of 1762, the Susquehannah Company convinced Connecticut families to relocate from the noisy swell of Connecticut towns to the free and open banks of the Susquehanna River. There were a few tentative settlements and retreats before a stable settlement began to take hold.

Large, toothy shad swam lazily in the river, easy to pick up in bare hands. The bottomland of the overflowing river was rich and deep, free of the rocks that plagued the settlers of granite-bound New England. Relocated Connecticut settlers began to work the land, raising rough log cabins and barns in the warm and fruitful valley.

As they moved into the area, the Europeans startled the Delaware, who reminded the Pennsylvanians that they were told no Whites would build there.

Initially, the Pennsylvanians did not act.

They had every intention to act.

Governor James Hamilton of Pennsylvania wrote two very persuasive missives to the state of Connecticut, warning against the terrible consequences should the Delaware and Iroquois follow through on threats to remove the interlopers by force.

In early October 1763, he wrote a proclamation to be read to the Yankee settlers in person by the Pennsylvania militia. The leader of the militia, Captain Asher Clayton, commanded a force of eighty men, whose orders from Governor Hamilton were to require the Connecticut families to vacate the premises immediately. Then the crops and homes were to be torched. If the settlers did not comply, the ringleaders were to be rounded up and taken to jail and the names of as many of the settlers as possible taken, so they could be prosecuted by law.

The time was exceptionally fraught, as Teedyuscung had been immolated in his home in April 1763, when twenty dwellings mysteriously burst into flames at the same moment. This attack on the Delaware was blamed on the Connecticut settlers. There is speculation that the killing of Teedyuscung was orchestrated by the Haudenosaunee, who were unhappy with his affect and his growing influence, and that they convinced his followers the Connecticut settlers had set the houses ablaze.[16] There was also speculation that this assault was orchestrated by the Pennsylvanians, who wanted to inspire the Delaware to remove the Yankees for them.

The Delaware blamed the Yankees and plotted revenge.

Chapter 3

AWLS IN THEIR EYE SOCKETS

O n October 15, 1763, Captain Thomas Bull, son of Teedyuscung, led a retaliatory attack on the Connecticut Yankees. Twenty men were massacred, ten of them in horrible fashion, their eyes stuck with awls and spears, arrows and pitchforks thrust into their bodies. One woman was suspended by hinges through her hands and roasted alive.

The attackers rushed out of the forest, their faces painted red and black, their cries echoing off the hills above the Susquehanna River as they fell on the unsuspecting settlers. Children watched with horror as a mother was roasted. Men, women and children ran into the woods, screaming and crying.

Two men were immediately scalped and several were chased down in the woods and dragged back to the fields where they had been working in the October sunshine. Bloody streaks colored the Susquehanna.

The Connecticut settlers John and Emanuel Hoover were building a chimney when they were forced to join the captives.[17] Several other adult and child prisoners were herded up the hills from the valley, as the attackers blended back into the woodlands.

The bodies of the dead were found two days later by the force that had been sent by Governor Hamilton, led by Captain Asher Clayton. They buried the dead, burned any remaining corn and other provisions, and set the nascent village of primitive log homes afire.

Noah Hopkins, a wealthy resident of Dutchess County in New York, was visiting the Wyoming Valley when the attack occurred. He was pursued

The Wyoming Massacre. Painting by F.O.C. Darley. 1905. *Collection of Stephen B. Killian, Esq.*

but hid in a hollow log until darkness. After wandering for five days, he returned to the Yankee settlement and reported, "All was desolation there; crops destroyed, cattle gone and the smoldering ruins of cabins were the only things visible....The stillness of death prevailed."[18]

The nearby Wyalusing mission was temporarily relocated to Philadelphia by the Moravians for the protection of the Delaware. The tribe remained there for fifteen months, "suffering untold hardships, insulted and reviled by mobs, decimated by disease, scorned alike by whites and Indians, a gazing stock both by reproaches and afflictions, yet they continued stedfast in their faith."[19]

By 1765 the Delaware survivors, having lost half their members, returned to Wyalusing, but according to one author, members of the tribe were no longer interested in a life "devoted to labor and the cultivation of the earth, and the restraints imposed by a settled, regulated society."[20] By 1772, the mission was abandoned, with the remainder of the Moravian Delaware moving to Ohio.

Chapter 4

GREAT MEN

*G*reat men was a term used by the kidnappers to refer to the community leaders who were behind the kidnapping. As backcountry ruffians living by their wits and the generosity of relatives, the Connecticut Yankees used the moniker as a term of respect.

These young kidnappers and their immediate relatives had come to the Wyoming Valley from various parts of New England but primarily from Connecticut, with a promise of land from the Susquehannah Company. By obtaining land, they hoped to become gentry who could meaningfully participate in town and church affairs, build schools for their children and vote. Backcountry settlers have long been celebrated by historians, who generally portray them as tough and persistent, hardworking and resilient:

> *They were not the effeminate sons of wealthy parents, who had been reared in the lap of luxury....They were the hardy, active, and ambitious sons of New Englanders, and in the exercise of the independent, self-reliant spirit which they had inherited from their sires, they left their paternal roofs and sought homes in this valley, far away in the untamed wilderness of what was then the west. A few brought with them their wives and children, and came with oxen and carts, bringing a few indispensable articles of household furniture and driving a few domestic animals. Most of them, however, came on foot, with knapsacks on their backs, rifles on their shoulders, and axes in their hands....They followed Indian trails, threaded forests and swamps, and climbed over mountains,*

Settlers traveled long distances with oxen and carts. *Original drawing by Kathleen A. Earle.*

camping in squads in the roads by night…and having selected their locations commenced their preparations for the future.[21]

Men like Colonel Pickering had been born into land and wealth, but this was still not the norm for many of the descendants of those arriving from the streets and fields of Europe.

According to Paul Moyer in *Wild Yankees: The Struggle for Independence along Pennsylvania's Revolutionary Frontier* (2007), the *great men* behind the kidnappers included New Englanders affiliated with the Susquehannah and Delaware Companies of Connecticut and with land speculators in other areas such as New York. Among the New Yorkers he mentions are Caleb Benton of Hillsdale, Joseph Hamilton of Hudson and Zerah Beach of Amenia. These three helped to convert the Susquehannah Company into an organization geared not only toward land speculation but toward insurgency, in which the land, once acquired, had to be defended. Also under this system, power was based on the decisions of specific shareholders, rather than on the votes of all.

As determined by the Pennsylvania authorities, the men behind the treasonous activities of the Wild Yankees were John Franklin, Zerah Beach, John Jenkins and

John McKinstry. These four were the subject of a warrant issued on September 26, 1787, to arrest them and bring them to Philadelphia. Colonel John McKinstry, affiliated with New York's Genesee Land Company, is mentioned tangentially in stories of the kidnapping, as is Zerah Beach. Both Franklin and Jenkins, however, took an outsized role in what became known as the Yankee-Pennamite Wars. Jenkins and Franklin were descendants of Englishmen who had immigrated to New England, obtained land and status and had not lost it over time, as had some of the fathers and grandfathers of the kidnappers.

JOHN FRANKLIN

John Franklin was the primary focus of Colonel Pickering's ire. His jailing led to the kidnapping.

Born on September 26, 1749, Franklin was the son of John Franklin Sr., alleged to be a man of wealth and standing in Canaan, Connecticut. John Sr. was an early shareholder in the Susquehannah Company but never visited his land in the Wyoming Valley.

David Craft, in his 1878 *History of Bradford County, Pennsylvania*, cites an incident from John Jr.'s youth to demonstrate what an intelligent and observant child he was. John did not pay attention one Sunday in church, relates Craft, but spent much of the sermon staring at the ceiling. His father, upon returning home, told John that he was going to get a severe thrashing for not paying attention at church and staring at the rafters during the sermon. John asked his father if he could remember the sermon, and then named the text and reiterated the main points. He then told his father how many beams and rafters there were in the meetinghouse. He did not get a thrashing.

A week after his marriage to Lydia Doolittle in 1774, John Franklin Jr. established a home in Plymouth Township in the Wyoming Valley; the following year he went alone to one of the three lots his father owned on the banks of Huntington Creek. In ten months he cleared four acres and built a log cabin, and he and Lydia established a home there in the wilderness, seven or eight miles from their nearest neighbor at the Susquehanna River.

Franklin was described as a tall, muscular man with a florid complexion and light hair, who impressed people with his intelligence, manner and tireless efforts on their behalf.[22]

When the American Revolution broke out, he was commissioned an ensign of the Twenty-Fourth Regiment of Connecticut Militia. He missed the Revolutionary Battle of Wyoming in July 1778 because his company was so scattered that they did not make it to the battle on time, arriving only to help the survivors. Shortly after this, in November of that year, Lydia contracted smallpox and died. Franklin took his children home to Connecticut in a cart pulled by oxen, with a cow tied to the back by her horns. He and the three children traveled this way for 260 miles through the wilderness.[23] He then returned to Wyoming and joined with the men and families who remained. He was made captain of the Salem and Huntington Company, Twenty-Fourth Regiment, and elected a justice of the peace. When General John Sullivan's campaign against the Iroquois was organized in 1779, Franklin volunteered. He was subsequently badly wounded in the shoulder by Haudenosaunee braves at Hogback Hill (Chemung) early in Sullivan's march.[24]

Portrait of John Franklin. *Stanley Jones, photographer; HABS.*

Over the next decade Franklin played a major role in defending the rights of the Connecticut Yankees against the claims of Pennsylvania. When Pickering arrived in the Wyoming Valley to end the hostilities, Franklin was center stage.

> *For two months he was engaged night and day. Riding up and down the valley, visiting from house to house, talking to little knots and gatherings of the people, writing letters to the prominent men of eastern New York and of New England, making frequent trips eastward, he was using all his energy and his powerful influence in opposition to Pickering and his supporters.*[25]

About a year before the kidnapping, and right before Franklin was captured, Thomas Wigton testified that "Franklin in particular said that he would Spill his blood in the Defence of the half Share men."[26]

In September 1787, the posse sent to capture Franklin, Jenkins, Beach and McKinstry was specifically instructed to capture Franklin and not to jeopardize his capture by pursuing the others.

Franklin's status as a *great man*, it may be surmised, was as much for his leadership skills and his loyalty to the Yankees as it was for his wealth and prestige.

JOHN JENKINS

John Jenkins Jr. (1751–1827) took an active role in the taking of Colonel Pickering. In his deposition after the kidnapping, Daniel Earl stated:

> *John Jenkins of Exeter (usually called major Jenkins)…proposed to me the taking of colonel Pickering as the way to get Franklin out of jail; and said he would give lands to the boys who should do it, and particularly promised to give me a right at Tioga if I would undertake it; and he afterwards sent up a certificate to me to entitle me to a right there. He also said he could sell his own right at Tioga for fifty dollars and that he would sell it, & the boys should have the money among them to make a frolic and that he would stand by us.*[27]

The Jenkins family first arrived in the Plymouth Colony; as Quakers, they did not quite fit in. John Jenkins Sr., father of the John Jenkins discussed here, was born in 1727 in East Greenwich, Rhode Island. John Sr. and his brothers Stephen, Palmer and Jonathan, along with his son John, were all proprietors of the Susquehannah Company of Connecticut. John Jenkins Sr. was one of the first Yankees to explore the Wyoming Valley in 1753 and was one of the signers of the land sale agreement with the Haudenosaunee in 1754. He was the head of the settlement during the massacre in 1763 and was driven out, only to return in 1769 with forty more Connecticut settlers, known as the First Forty. These included his eldest son, John, one of the *great men*, who was eighteen at the time.

A schoolteacher, surveyor, justice of the peace and judge of the first county court of Wyoming, John Jenkins the elder was elected to the legislature of Connecticut five times. His death was attributed to a skirmish with the Pennamites:

> *Driven out by the Pennamites in May 1784, in a cold spring storm, he took a severe cold, which taking the form of rheumatism and settling in a wound in his knee which he received from a ball at the taking of Louisburg in 1745, he suffered on until the month of November following, when he died, a victim of Pennamite injustice and cruelty.*[28]

His son John was born at Gardner's Lake in New London, Connecticut, on November 27, 1751. With his brothers Stephen (b. 1753) and Wilkes (b. 1767), he joined the ranks of those trying to defend Connecticut settlers' land claims.

Forty Fort, 1772–78. Centennial Jubilee and Old Home Week, Wilkes-Barre, Pennsylvania, 1906. *Collection of Luzerne County Historical Society (LCHS), Wilkes-Barre, Pennsylvania.*

In 1777, at the beginning of the American Revolution, Jenkins was taken prisoner and marched to the British stronghold at Niagara. He escaped and returned home in June 1778, just in time to warn the settlers in the Wyoming Valley about preparations for an upcoming invasion by the British, Tories and Iroquois.

Jenkins was in command of Forty Fort, named for the First Forty settlers, during the subsequent Battle of Wyoming. A year later he used the expertise he had gained through his capture and escape from the Iroquois to advise General Washington and guide General Sullivan's march.

Jenkins continued to take part in the American Revolution and was at the surrender of Cornwallis on October 17, 1781. He returned home in 1782 to find the Pennamites and Yankees still trying to force each other out of the valley and doubtless was beside his father through the difficult siege by the Pennamites in 1784, which ultimately led to his father's death.

John Jr. was described by Frederick Cook, in his 1887 narrative about Sullivan's march, as a surveyor, schoolteacher, constable, farmer, merchant, ironmonger and agent for the Susquehannah Company at Wyoming. He married Bethia Harris and had eight children.

In 1788 he was elected lieutenant colonel of the local Wyoming Valley Militia. By then, Colonel Pickering had been appointed to the Wyoming

Valley to sort out the Yankee-Pennamite wars. In regard to the election of Jenkins and other militia officers, Pickering stated that he believed the men elected as officers were elected "not to support, but, in proper time, to oppose, the government of Pennsylvania."[29]

After the kidnapping, John Jenkins was a surveyor of the Phelps and Gorham Purchase in upstate New York. He did not stay in New York but returned to Exeter in the Wyoming Valley, where he died in 1827.

ETHAN ALLEN

Statue of Ethan Allen.
Photograph collection of LCHS.

Among early land speculators in the Wyoming Valley was Ethan Allen of Vermont. Like the Yankees, Allen was originally from Connecticut. Several Yankees were from Litchfield, where Allen was born in 1737. His family moved from Litchfield to Cornwall when he was two years old. In about 1765 Allen moved to Vermont, then called the New Hampshire Grants. This territory was under dispute by the colonies of New York and New Hampshire, and Allen's Green Mountain Boys were instrumental in the eventual creation of the state of Vermont out of the disputed territory.

Historical records show that Allen was present in Wyoming before the kidnapping, arguing and agitating on the side of the Connecticut claimants. It was said that he appeared with his Green Mountain Boys "in regimentals and cocked hat," for the purpose of creating a new state.[30]

Allen's help was happily embraced by the Yankees. In 1992, a local Pennsylvania historian stated that "Colonel Ethan Allen, the Green Mountain hero, came from Vermont and built a cabin by the side of the spring [in Tunkhannock] and lived there a short time, occasionally appearing at Wilkes-Barre in full regimentals."[31] By 1786, rumors of his offered assistance reached a fever pitch, and this letter appeared in the *Connecticut Courant*:

> *It is reported that Ethan Allen, seized with the* divine flame *of propagating* his gospel, *has lately paid a visit to the Wyoming settlers, to whom he preached some of his* pious lectures, *to their wonderful edification. The* disinterestedness *of this* holy man *cannot be too highly celebrated; as, for the* very trifling *recompense of* two townships, *each six miles square, he has with wonderful magnanimity offered to head* his elect *against the* infidels *of Pennsylvania.*[32]

Allen's plan to help the Connecticut settlers form a new state in the middle of Pennsylvania never came to fruition, however, and he returned to Vermont.

TIMOTHY PICKERING

Franklin and Jenkins, although they had similar backgrounds to Pickering, did not share his status as one of the *notable* men of the nascent United States.

Pickering's ancestral background was inauspicious. The first Pickering to arrive in New England was a carpenter, who was admitted as an inhabitant of Salem, Massachusetts, in 1637. According to Gerard H. Clarfield in *Timothy Pickering and the American Republic* (1980), each generation strived for status, establishing themselves as leading citizens of Salem. Timothy's grandfather John Pickering served as a representative to the Massachusetts General Court. His father, Timothy Sr., enlarged the extensive family landholdings and became deacon of the Third Congregational Church in Salem. Timothy Jr. was born in the ancestral home in Salem on July 17, 1745. He graduated from Harvard College in 1763 and received a master of arts degree in 1766. He studied law and joined the Massachusetts bar in 1768.

Despite his elite education and impressive background, Pickering was described by Clarfield as "one of the principal villains of early American history."[33] Clarfield had wanted, in writing Pickering's biography, to resuscitate Pickering's reputation, he stated, but Pickering's villainy was convincingly demonstrated by the sources mined for the book. Clarfield characterizes Pickering as a "young man on the make" who "never made it."

Pickering was a tall, gangly youth. His father was a rigid and overbearing deacon who "cloaked himself in righteousness in order to enjoy more fully the discomfiture of others."[34] He sent his son to Harvard when he was fourteen years old. Of interest is that Pickering carried a pound of chocolate with him to Harvard; this was one of the items he requested the kidnappers fetch for him when he was their captive in the woods of Tunkhannock. Although he had a fondness for chocolate, he allegedly did not like Harvard.

In Salem, Pickering became colonel of the local militia and worked to improve the discipline of the troops. He also got into disputes with local officials, such as the local doctor, whom he challenged to a duel, and the local minister, which led him to leave the church. He affiliated himself with the rich and powerful men in town, who were initially the Tories. By 1770 Pickering had renounced the Tories and joined the American Revolutionary contingent. He was subsequently accused in an anonymous

Timothy Pickering, 1745–1829. Unknown artist. *Collection of LCHS.* *Photograph by Stan Fox.*

newspaper column "of the lowest form of political opportunism and [the author] hoped that he might fully 'enjoy the wished for applause and reap the virtuous satisfaction of having bartered honesty for interest.'"[35] His father remained a Tory for the rest of his life.

Physically awkward, shy and insecure around women, Pickering married Rebecca White, a woman nine years his junior, in 1776. When Rebecca was six months pregnant, he responded to a call for volunteers to join General George Washington in New York. Shortly after returning to Rebecca and his young son in 1777, he was offered the position of adjutant general. He then held administrative positions in the revolutionary effort, serving on the Board of War and as quartermaster general.

As quartermaster general, Pickering was described by one of his colleagues as "arrogant and self-righteous without being particularly bright or efficient… quick to make moral judgments and snap decisions based too frequently on inadequate information."[36] Feuds with General Washington regarding the provision of supplies to the troops made Pickering angry and resentful. His differences with Washington continued through the end of the Revolution.

A few months before the Treaty of Paris on September 3, 1783, Pickering, bitter and tired from his life of public service so far, formed a company with Samuel Hodgdon to provide European goods to the United States. However, there were so many newly created merchants and so little business that the company failed. Pickering's continuing salary as quartermaster kept bankruptcy at bay.

In 1784, he and Hodgdon became land speculators, buying twenty thousand acres in what is now northeastern Pennsylvania. Of these, 450 acres were located in the land under dispute between the Connecticut Yankees and the Pennamites. Pickering reportedly decided that settling the dispute would increase the value of all his holdings in the area and convinced the leaders of Pennsylvania to send him to Wilkes-Barre to bring peace to the valley.

His conditions for undertaking this task were that (1) a new county would be established in the Wyoming district, where the Connecticut people would have autonomy and control of their own courts of justice, (2) Pennsylvania would pass legislation legitimizing the land titles of Connecticut claimants who had settled land before 1782, the year of the Trenton decision and (3) Pickering would be appointed to several local offices that would produce substantial income as the population of the area grew.

Pickering's plan did not address the approximately three hundred men and their families who had come to the valley since 1782. This included several families of the kidnappers, who had recently acquired land from the Susquehannah Company.

In keeping with their agreement with Pickering, Pennsylvania created Luzerne County[37] from part of Northumberland County on September 25, 1786, and shortly thereafter appointed Pickering to every important county office they could find, in order to meet his requirements for taking the post. In January 1787 Pickering moved to Wilkes-Barre as a public official empowered to handle local affairs.

A year and a half later, he was kidnapped.

While the Wyoming Valley was overrun with rough men and primitive farms, Philadelphia, a mere 150 miles away, might as well have been located in Europe. At the time of the kidnapping, Philadelphia was seething with new optimism and wealth, having just defeated Britain and created the United States of America. Subduing a few disgruntled settlers in the backwoods of the Wyoming Valley must have seemed an easy task for the *great men* of Philadelphia.

Chapter 5

WILD YANKEES

Among the soldiers under Clayton who discovered the gory scene of the first Wyoming massacre was Lazarus Stewart of Hanover, a backwoods settlement along the Pennsylvania border of what is now Maryland. Stewart was notorious for his alleged violence and ignorance of norms of civilized behavior. In the 1760s, incursions against colonial settlements by Native people gave Stewart and his cohort an excuse for carnage on a horrific scale. Native men, women and children, friendly or hostile, were butchered indiscriminately. This gang of unruly, ragged and relatively recent Scots and Irish immigrants was called the Paxton Boys, for the town in Pennsylvania where they lived.

A dominant force in that community was the Paxton Presbyterian Church, formed in 1740; many of the Paxton Boys are believed to have been parishioners. The pastor of the church, John Elder, was the commander of the Paxton Boys, also known as the Paxton Rangers.

Clayton was a leader of one of two companies appointed to defend the frontier community against tribal incursions in July of 1763. Governor James Hamilton of Pennsylvania appointed Clayton; the other leader, Timothy Green, a parishioner of Paxton Presbyterian, was chosen by Pastor Elder. One of the first tasks of the Paxton Boys was to help Clayton's militia bury the dead and burn the houses after the destruction of the little Connecticut Yankee community.

Just a few months after the massacre at Wyoming, on December 14, 1763, fifty-seven men armed with guns and hatchets brutally murdered and scalped members of the Conestoga tribe, who had, according to Benjamin Franklin, welcomed the first Pennsylvanian settlers with gifts of venison, corn and skins. The Conestoga were friendly neighbors and protectorates of the Quaker community in Pennsylvania. At the time of the attack on the village, only seven Conestoga were at home: "Wa-a-shen, also called George Sock; Tee-Kau-ley, also known as Harry; Kannenquas, a middle-aged woman; Tea-wonsha-i-ong, or Sally, an older woman; her adopted child, Tong-quas, or Chrisly...Ess-canesh, a young boy...[and] Sheehays or Sohais, often called Old Sheehays."[38]

The residents of nearby Lancaster, horrified and saddened by the butchering of their friends, collected the remaining members of the Conestoga and put them in a workhouse (prison) for their own protection. On December 27, fifty White attackers broke open the workhouse, and men, women and children were scalped, hacked and cut to pieces in the prison yard.

Benjamin Franklin wrote a long discourse decrying this crime. He referred to the perpetrators as "persons unknown," but later authors blamed the

Depiction of the murder of the Conestoga, with the Paxton boys in top hats. 1841. Lithograph from James Witmer's *Events in Indian History*.

Paxton Boys. The names of the murderers have been difficult to confirm, although Stewart and others have been implicated. According to Stewart himself, the Pennsylvania authorities ordered his arrest for this outrage. But outcry from settlers, both Pennamite and Yankee, kept the Paxton Boys out of jail and free to continue their murderous rampage.

As with much of history, there are two views regarding the complicated Lazarus Stewart. Egle, in 1898, presented the following view of Lazarus through the eyes of his wife, Martha Epsy Stewart. Egle also reiterated Stewart's participation in the murder of the Conestoga:

> *Few have any conception of the horrors constantly menacing the Scotch-Irish settlements, and at last when the Indian war ceased, the persecution of her heroic husband endued her heart with that womanly loyalty which buoyed the patriot and nerved his arm for the right.…Lazarus was well grounded in the essentials of a good English education and was raised a farmer. In 1775… he raised a company for the defense of the frontiers and performed valiant service as a ranger. The part Captain Stewart took in the transactions at Conestoga and Lancaster in the destruction of the vagabond and murderous Indians there kept and protected, in December 1763, made him a prominent personage in the history of Pennsylvania during that period.…So highly esteemed and appreciated was Lazarus Stewart, that he was commissioned lieutenant-colonel of the Second regiment of Connecticut militia.*[39]

After the massacre of the Conestoga, Stewart and others manufactured a narrative in which the Conestoga were harboring the dangerous murderer of a Ranger's mother, and when the Rangers tried to arrest the murderer, the Conestoga attacked the Rangers. The murderer escaped, and the resulting slaughter of everyone at the workhouse inadvertently killed both the friendly and the unfriendly. Pastor Elder claimed for years that he had tried to stop the Paxton Boys from murdering the Conestoga.

In 1769 Stewart joined the Connecticut Yankees and was among those who sent a petition to the Pennsylvania Assembly complaining about the colony's land policies. Later that year he began negotiations with the Susquehannah Company of Connecticut to destroy the Pennamite settlements in return for shares of land. This proposal was eagerly accepted by the Company, which had just sent over two hundred new settlers from Connecticut to the area under the leadership of Major John Durkee. Durkee was joined by Captain Zebulon Butler. Both would become leaders in the forcible ripping of the new colonies from the bosom of England.

When the Paxton Boys traveled to the Wyoming Valley to join the Connecticut Yankees, they added a new element to what had been a relatively benign engagement of Pennsylvania and Connecticut protagonists. Prior to Stewart's involvement, disputes between the Connecticut and Pennsylvania settlers were handled relatively amicably. Landowners were told to leave, or taken to court, instead of having their homes and possessions destroyed. Now, engagements between Connecticut and Pennsylvania settlers were ratcheted up to a new level of hostility and rage. Stewart and his men showed no mercy and gave no ground to the Philadelphia men and the settlers they were protecting. Lazarus provided an exciting role model for the rabble hoard of young Wild Yankees, encouraging their more violent impulses while destroying the homes and lives of Pennsylvanian interlopers. Yankees leveled the homes of Pennamites, plundered their possessions and killed their livestock. They dressed and behaved like warlike Natives, complete with drumbeating, blood-curdling shouts, the application of blackface and feather headdresses. The Pennamites were equally vicious in their attempts to rid the valley of the Yankees, and dispossession and displacement were commonplace. Reports of their behavior in the 1770s portrayed Tories, many of whom were also Pennamites, "as people who possessed the same savagery, mercilessness, and brutality that supposedly characterized Indians."[40] The lands of the Susquehanna became known as the Dark and Bloody Valley.

The wave of the death struggle swept back and forth; literally charges and retreats and counter charges; captures and expulsions and then recaptures and again repulsed; the swarming immigrant this year, the sad exodus the next; the victory today, the bloody massacre almost sure to swiftly follow. The scythe of death moved its winrows in the ranks and eagerly came others in the place of the dead. What destiny hung in the balance, so long suspended by a single hair! This was something of the alembic that distilled the remarkable manhood that has inscribed high in the temple of the immortals the names of most of the first settlers of what is now Luzerne County.[41]

Chapter 6

THE HAUDENOSAUNEE (IROQUOIS)

Kitchi-Manitou has given us a different understanding.
—Red Jacket[42]

A ny history of this area must include a discussion of the Haudenosaunee, called Iroquois by the Whites, whose relationship with the European settlers has been underreported and misrepresented since first contact.

When the Europeans arrived, the Iroquois were a powerful nation of independent people and a confederacy of five tribes: the Mohawk, Oneida, Onondaga, Cayuga and Seneca. A sixth tribe, the Tuscarora, sought refuge with the Iroquois after being defeated by colonial forces in 1712. Official recognition as the sixth nation of the Iroquois Confederacy was conferred on them in 1722. The Haudenosaunee had already defeated or adopted the populations of several other tribes, including the Cat People, Huron, Neutrals, Erie and Algonquin of the Great Lakes area. Southeastern tribal groups who sought refuge among the Iroquois and were adopted included the Saponi and Tutelo from Virginia; Nanicokes from Chesapeake Bay; and the Delaware.

The Haudenosaunee occupied much of the area of what is now New York State. Their territory extended up into Canada and through the south of present-day New York to at least the Susquehanna River, in what is now Pennsylvania. In 1650 the total population of the Haudenosaunee was about 25,000. This included 10,000 Seneca, 3,000 Cayuga, 4,000

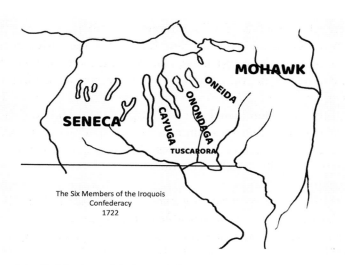

The Six Members of the Iroquois Confederacy 1722

Location of the Six Members of the Iroquois Confederacy in 1722. *Drawing by Kathleen A. Earle.*

Onondaga, 3,000 Oneida and 5,000 Mohawk.[43] The population in 1791 had shrunk to about 4,500, including 1,900 Seneca, 400 Cayuga, 500 Onondaga, 600 Oneida, 300 Tuscarora, and 800 Mohawk.[44] The 2010 US census lists 48,000 Iroquois, but it is unclear whether these are enrolled or not enrolled.[45]

The culture of White and Black New Englanders differed dramatically from that of the Haudenosaunee, who predated them in that area of the world by thousands of years. As documented by Rupert Ross in *Dancing with a Ghost* (2006), the culture was and is characterized by true freedom of individuals, who are taught from an early age to make their own decisions. Children's misbehavior is tolerated; if a child truly shows evil intent, he or she is punished by temporary banishment. In the old days, children who were temporarily banished had ashes put on their face and were ignored by everyone around them, signifying their exclusion from the group.

It is a way of life steeped in both mysticism and practicality among members of both the historical and the modern Haudenosaunee. Ceremonies are still held to purge evil spirits from individuals who have been affected by outside forces that invade our minds and our bodies. At a powwow,[46] drummers attach a powerful amplifier to a two-hundred-year-old drum to make the sound reverberate more loudly. The Haudenosaunee have mastered the art of keeping the old traditions but using modern techniques and inventions to amplify (in this case, literally) the message.

When tens of thousands of White immigrants crossed the Atlantic and planted themselves on the coast of New England in the early seventeenth century, they brought their pigs, cows, children and many of their diseases with them. Parenthetically, they also brought dandelions, a current reminder of these persistent people whose roots were hard to destroy and whose pale and fuzzy faces have dominated the landscape of the United States ever since. The shock of seeing these unusual beings continued into the mid-nineteenth century, as settlers moved west. In the late nineteenth century, Jaime, a Navajo, described such an encounter:

> *One day I saw a man coming along with big white whiskers all over his face. The skin that showed was around his eyes, just a little bit. I had never seen a white man before. I ran away home and told the people I had seen something out there coming toward the sheep. It looked like a man, I said, but had wool all over its face.*[47]

The Iroquois Confederacy was—and still is, among traditional adherents—held together by its constitution, the Iroquois Book of the Great Law. The Great Law was based on the concept of the Great Peace, to be overseen and enforced by the original Five Nations. Decisions of the Iroquois are traditionally first debated by sachems within the five member tribes and then at the Council Fire of the Onondaga, the center of the Confederacy, until absolute unanimity is reached. Sachems belong to one of the fifty maternal families in which that title is hereditary.[48]

Behind these men are the women. Traditional Haudenosaunee society is matriarchal and matrilineal, based on a system of familial clans. This tradition exists alongside the election of leaders as prescribed by the United States federal government in 1934 as part of the Indian Reorganization Act.[49] Traditional clan mothers preside over the household and also make ultimate decisions on social and political matters. The matriarchs choose the fifty sachems of the Iroquois and can remove them for misbehavior, in a ceremony called de-horning, in which deer antlers were traditionally removed from the head of a deposed sachem.

According to Haudenosaunee history, a sachem was traditionally different from a chief. The word *sachem* refers to one of the original fifty hereditary leaders of the Iroquois. This title is given when someone is elevated to the office and takes the name of one of the original sachems. Thus, Red Jacket, the famous Seneca orator, was originally named O-te-ti-an-i, meaning "always ready"; when he was elevated to sachem, he was

Traditional Cayuga headdress made by Jacob Thomas, Jr. *Photograph by Kathleen A. Earle.*

given one of the eight sachem names of the Seneca, "Sa-go-ye-wat-ha," or "keeper awake."

Chiefs included celebrated orators, wise men and military leaders. Red Jacket, in fact, was such a great orator that he was almost not elevated to sachem, as the sachems are supposed to be modest and to eschew public recognition, their duties confined primarily to the affairs of peace. It is interesting to note that during the Battle of Wyoming, Red Jacket was at the back of the attackers and did not kill anyone. He was later sometimes kidded for his lack of interest in battle, but this was seen as a virtue as well. One of the most famous Mohawk warriors, Joseph Brant, never acquired the title of sachem. Over time, the term *sachem* has become synonymous with the term *chief*.

Early attitudes of Europeans toward the Haudenosaunee were tinged with awe. They admired the Haudenosaunee for their self-confidence, civility, eloquence when speaking in council, sharing of time and their decorum, which required, for example, that any speaker be allowed to complete his speech without interruption, after which the listeners would withdraw for rest and reflection before responding.[50] They were a democratic people, in that their chosen leaders were the same as anyone else, attaining their status by their skill and valor in battle, dignity of bearing and eloquence.

The concepts of relationship and reciprocity were central to historic Haudenosaunee culture, and the exchange of wampum was an integral part of maintaining relationships among the Iroquois and with those outside the culture. The Great Law was originally transmitted and enforced based on an oral tradition that used wampum belts as visual cues for each law or regulation.

Wampum consisted of beads cut from seashells that were ground, polished and bored through the center with a hand drill. Some beads were made from the quahog, acquired as tribute to the Iroquois from the Natives of Long Island, New York; others were from the white conch shell and the purple spot in a clam shell. The purple and white beads, arranged in various designs, were used in ceremonies and diplomacy, such as council and civil proceedings, installment of chiefs and notifications or agreements regarding war and peace.[51] Wampum was regarded as an essential part of official transactions, and no chief would listen to a report until it was officially confirmed with a wampum belt carried by a runner; treaties were ignored unless accompanied by wampum.

The two-row wampum belt consisted of about a foot-long band of white beads with two rows of purple beads running parallel to each other from one end of the band to the other. Considered a treaty by the Haudenosaunee with the Dutch settlers in 1613, it signified a canoe and ship going down a river beside each other, not touching or interfering with each other: the equal but non-intersecting destinies of the Iroquois and the Whites.[52] In 2013, the four hundredth anniversary of the Two-Row Wampum Treaty, the Onondaga Nation partnered with organizations in New York State to celebrate and renew the treaty. Two lines of boats navigated down the Hudson River, side by side. On one side of the Hudson were White and Black Americans in small boats, and on the other were members of the Haudenosaunee in canoes.[53]

During the seventeenth and eighteenth centuries, the Iroquois traded, warred and sometimes fought alongside different factions of the Europeans. Meanwhile, the continued encroachment of colonial settlers into Iroquois territory exacerbated tensions.

The Haudenosaunee were participants in the attacks on settlers in the Wyoming Valley in the 1700s, including the Wyoming massacres of 1763 and 1778. People were kidnapped at these battles and their fate, as described in captivity narratives from the eighteenth century, is instructive when trying to understand both the Iroquois culture and the relationship between colonial and Native people. Kidnapping and adoption were common among the Haudenosaunee following raids of White settlements. Haudenosaunee captors watched their captives carefully in order to determine whether to kill or adopt their prisoners.

Those adopted were frequently the replacements for warriors lost in battle; they became accepted members of the Haudenosaunee. Later, adoption and the conferring of a Haudenosaunee name were considered an opportunity to show acceptance and honor to a valued friend or colleague.

Among the Connecticut Yankees who first settled the Wyoming Valley in 1763 was Jonathan Slocum, the father of famed captive Frances Slocum. Frances was kidnapped by the Delaware on November 2, 1778, along with a neighbor boy and a Black servant girl. Frances was given the name Little Bear Woman and eventually married a Miami warrior.

Prisoners from the Wyoming Valley. Albert Bobbett, wood-engraver; F.O.C. Darley, artist. 1877. *Collection of Stephen B. Killian, Esq.*

From the Wyoming Valley, Frances's captors would have herded prisoners up the hills leading north and west from the Susquehanna River. Stories of captives from that time include tales of traveling great distances through dense forests.

Mary Jemison, who was abducted with nine others in 1755 from her home in western Pennsylvania, described her journey to the land of the Seneca as a thirteen-year-old:

> *On our march that day, an Indian went behind us with a whip, with which he frequently lashed the children, to make them keep up. In this manner we traveled till dark, without a mouthful of food or a drop of water....Whenever the little children cried for water, the Indians would make then drink urine, or go thirsty. At night they encamped in the woods, without fire and without shelter, where we were watched with the greatest vigilance. Extremely fatigued, and very hungry, we were compelled to lie upon the ground, without supper or a drop of water to satisfy the cravings of our appetites.*[54]

Mary spent the next twenty-nine years in Little Beard's Town as a member of the Seneca, who gave her the name Deh-he-wa-mis, which means "a pretty girl, a handsome girl, or a pleasant, good thing." Her Seneca husband, Hiadagoo (also spelled Hiakatoo), later fought on the British side in the Battle of Wyoming.

Another adoptee, Father Poncet, who was taken by the Mohawks in 1653, described the adoption ceremony as his becoming a literal replacement for a dead relative:

> *So soon as I entered her cabin she began to sing the song of the dead, in which she was joined by her two daughters. I was standing near the fire during these mournful dirges; they made me sit upon a sort of table slightly raised, and then I understood I was in the place of the dead, for whom these women renewed the last mourning, to bring the deceased to life again in my person, according to their customs.*[55]

Mary Jemison was adopted by two Seneca women to replace their brother who had been killed in battle. In an interview in 1823, Mary stated, "I was ever considered and treated by them as a real sister, the same as though I had been born of their mother."[56]

Mary married two chiefs and had seven children. She and all other adoptees of the Iroquois Nation were "freed" on October 22, 1784, with the Treaty of Fort Stanwix between the United States and the Iroquois Confederacy. Under this treaty, all prisoners, White or Black, who had been abducted by the Haudenosaunee were to be "delivered up." Mary "resolved not to accept her freedom, but to spend the remainder of her days with the Seneca, where she knew she had affectionate relatives and many kind friends."[57]

After Mary had been discovered and celebrated by the Americans, she became known as the White Woman of the Genesee, and a statue stands in her honor in Letchworth State Park, Castile, New York.

Frances Slocum was five years old when she was kidnapped by the Delaware from her home near the Susquehanna.

She spent most of her life with the Delaware, and after the Treaty of Fort Stanwix, she and her tribe purposely evaded her discovery by her brothers, who searched diligently for her. In 1835, she was discovered, and a letter was written to the postmaster of Lancaster, Pennsylvania, where her relatives lived:

> [Frances is] *old and feeble and thinks she will not live long. These considerations induced her to give the present history of herself, which she*

The Capture of Frances Slocum. Lossing & Barritt, engraver. 1858. *Collection of Stephen B. Killian, Esq.*

would never do before, fearing that her kindred would come and force her
away. She has lived long and happy as an Indian and, but for her color,
would not be suspected of being anything else than such.[58]

The letter found its way to her biological nephew Joseph Slocum, and a party of Slocum relatives visited her in September 1837. They recognized Frances from an old childhood injury to her finger and "tried every means in our power to induce her to return with us…but such are her manners, her habits and customs, that I fear everything will prove ineffectual."[59]

Over the course of American history, the Iroquois have been portrayed as bloodthirsty savages. Although they frequently terrified the encroaching Whites and their Native neighbors, the Haudenosaunee were a warlike people only as was required for their own preservation. Children were taught how fight and how to torture prisoners; they were also taught how to withstand torture without flinching or crying out. Among themselves, and with Whites and Blacks whom they knew, the Haudenosaunee were and are non-judgmental and trusting. This attitude was reflected in various writings from the late eighteenth and early nineteenth centuries and is still reported by non-Natives with whom they come in contact.

People of European descent who visited the Iroquois and affiliated Nations early in the time of American history described with awe a society of true equals, whose people treated others as equals. The indigenous inhabitants of America provided an early example to the nascent United States of how to be truly free. As explained by a member of the Hurons to an early French ethnographer in the late seventeenth century:

> *We are born free and united brothers, each as much a great lord as the other, while you are all the slaves of one sole man. I am the master of my body, I dispose of myself, I do what I wish, I am the first and the last of my Nation…subject only to the great Spirit.*[60]

Chapter 7

BLOOD ON THE LAND

The early massacre of Connecticut settlers in 1763 had initially disrupted plans by Connecticut settlers to inhabit the Wyoming Valley, but the Susquehannah Company continued to encourage families to move there. As stated by the company in 1768, settlers were made proprietors of the land on the condition that they would remain in the valley and help to defend it against rival claimants. As encouragement, each family was given £200 to purchase provisions and supplies.[61]

From 1770 to 1790, control of the Wyoming Valley seesawed between the settlers from Connecticut and those from Pennsylvania. Farms and homes would be established, town meetings held, and then the whole community would be decimated once again. The Pennamites made hostile attacks on Yankee farms and settlers, and the Yankees did the same to the Pennamites, the two sides taking turns destroying each other's lands and livelihood.

The Haudenosaunee continued to interact with the burgeoning number of Whites overtaking the landscape. Individuals and families became friends, and many complicated relationships evolved.

During the intercolonial wars preceding the Revolution, most of the Haudenosaunee maintained neutrality. This began to change in 1746, with the British appointment of Sir William Johnson as commissary for Indian affairs and colonel of the forces to be raised out of the Six Nations. Johnson became a trusted friend and leader, primarily by the Mohawks. After the French, whom they had supported, were defeated by the British, the Seneca joined the alliance, and by the beginning of the Revolution the

Joseph Brant (1742–1807), 1786, Gilbert Stuart (1755–1828), oil on canvas, H: 30 x W: 25 in. Fenimore Art Museum, Cooperstown, New York. *Gift of Stephen C. Clark. N0199. 1961. Photograph by Richard Walker.*

Cayuga and Onondaga also joined, leaving the other two members of the Iroquois Confederacy, the Oneida and Tuscarora, primarily loyal to the Continentals.[62]

The British actively recruited Haudenosaunee to fight the colonial rebels, and these warriors made up a large contingent of the British forces, frequently outnumbering the British and Tories fighting alongside them.

The relationship of the Haudenosaunee to the British during the American Revolution may be illustrated by the story of Joseph Brant, leader of the Iroquois forces for most of the battles fought in that war. As a young man, Brant was taken from his Mohawk home in 1761 and sent to the Charity School of Lebanon, Connecticut, known as the Wheelock School after its founder, Dr. Eleazer Wheelock. The purpose of the school was to "teach, clothe, and board six children of the Six Nations." When he arrived at the school, Brant could only speak a little English, but he quickly learned not only English but also Latin and Greek. He was also fluent in all six tongues of the Iroquois Nations.

His mentor at the Mohawk Nation was Tiyanoga, who taught him that the British were friends to the Haudenosaunee. Joseph fought the French in the French and Indian War, beside Tiyanoga.

Sir William Johnson fathered two children with Joseph's sister, Molly Brant. As the revolution progressed, Brant became allied more with the British even than with his Haudenosaunee brothers.

A story that portrays the mixed heritage and training of Brant was told by Graymont (1972). According to her, Brant had a soft spot for fellow members of the Free and Accepted Masons.

In July 1779, with sixty Iroquois and twenty-seven Tories, Brant attacked the town of Minisink, near Goshen, New York. A prisoner, Captain John Wood, was about to be tomahawked by one of Brant's warriors when he inadvertently gave the Master Mason's sign of distress. Brant pushed the warrior aside and grasped the hand of Wood, giving the Master Mason's grip. Later he gave Wood his own blanket to sleep in. The next day Brant mentioned Freemasonry to Wood, who innocently told him he was not a Mason, not understanding that this was the reason his life had been spared. When Wood returned from captivity many years later, he joined the Freemasons.

Tories, or Loyalists, were loyal to the British. The Yankee settlers of the Wyoming Valley believed that some of their neighbors, including many of the Pennamites, were Tories. In January 1776, they set up a Committee of Inspection to identify Tories in their midst and informed them they would not be harmed if they adhered to the laws of Connecticut and the decrees of the new Continental Congress. Those who did not comply were harassed and their property seized. Many of the dispossessed Pennamites had indeed become Loyalists.

As the Revolution coalesced, the adult males from Connecticut in the Wyoming Valley were organized into the Twenty-Fourth Regiment, Connecticut Militia, with Colonel Nathan Denison as its leader. Two independent companies were placed under the command of Captains Robert Durkee and Samuel Ransom. However, they were immediately ordered to report to General Washington in New Jersey. Yankee patriots in the valley continued to join the Revolution, but when they did, they were sent to help out in battles far from home, leaving only women, boys and old men behind to defend their homes and relatives.

The battle in the Wyoming Valley on July 3, 1778, that came to be known as the Wyoming Massacre was anticipated by John Jenkins, who escaped from Iroquois captors who had sent him to Canada in 1777. As he made his way back through the Haudenosaunee homelands in June 1778, he noted extensive preparations for battle by the Haudenosaunee and British.

Jenkins reported what he had seen to Colonel Denison, and Denison sent him to make a full report to General Washington. Washington felt that his troops were needed elsewhere, and Jenkins went from there to implore Captains Ransom and Durkee of the Wyoming Company to leave their posts and return to defend their homes. When permission was withheld, they resigned and returned to the Valley to fight. Lieutenant Simon Spaulding took charge of the Wyoming Company, which, however, did not immediately return to Pennsylvania.

Jenkins returned with only four men: Ransom, Durkee and two other officers who had resigned as well, Lieutenants James Welles and Perrin Ross. However, they were without their full companies of about five hundred men.

By the end of June 1778, the situation at Wyoming was dire.

> *Everyone in the valley who could stand and walk was working to help with the fortifications, but the defenses were still pitiable. Long ago the cream of Wyoming's young men had been formed into the two strong companies that had then been withdrawn from the valley for use elsewhere in the war effort. Now, although there were still a number of able-bodied men here, there were mostly women and little children and old men who were working as much as twenty hours a day to strengthen defenses.*[63]

One of the valley's own, Zebulon Butler, requested leave from the Continental army and returned home, where he found a ragtag group of old men and boys, afraid for their lives.

The British leader John Butler (no relation to Zebulon Butler) found out from his spies that the Wyoming Valley was poorly defended and made its invasion a cornerstone of his plan to divide the north from the south, with the Susquehanna River as the dividing line.

At the Wyoming Valley battle the Haudenosaunee were the major fighting force. Miner (1845) stated that John Butler's army consisted of 400 British, made up of Colonel John Butler's Rangers, Sir John Johnson's Royal Greens and Tories from New York, New Jersey and Pennsylvania plus 600–700 Natives, totaling over 1,000 fighting men. Historians of the Haudenosaunee report that the British force consisted of 110 of Butler's Rangers and 464 Iroquois, mostly Seneca and Cayuga. Seneca allies of Butler, besides Mary Jemison's husband Hiadagoo, included Cornplanter, who was second in command, Little Beard, Little Billy, Farmer's Brother, Twenty Canoes, Jack Berry, Half Town and Red Jacket. Some of these warriors would become famous in later years. Other British allies who fought in the battle were Fish Carrier of the Cayuga; Sagwarithra, a sachem of the Tuscarora; and Gahkoondenoiya of the Onondaga.[64] The Seneca Handsome Lake, whom some regard as the spiritual leader of the Iroquois, also participated in the battle as a "common warrior…along with Blacksnake, Old Smoke, Farmer's Brother, and most of the other distinguished…Seneca."[65] The Mohawk Joseph Brant, although he was later accused of atrocities at the battle, was not there. He was in charge of the Cherry Valley attack in upstate New York the following November.

Little Beard was a well-known Seneca chief; Little Beard's Town (Dynnon-dah ga-eeh), near present-day Geneseo on the Genesee River, was a major Seneca village that was considered by some the capital of the western Iroquois. Mary Jemison spent most of her life there. The village was visited frequently by Brant and John Butler and was the place where many of the expeditions against the enemy Continental rebels were planned. Little Beard was regarded as a person of considerable importance to both the Haudenosaunee and the British, "fierce and cruel while on the warpath, in the councils of the tribe…a man of keen good sense and judgement, and his views carried with them great weight."[66] Haudenosaunee leaders were highly respected by those who knew them well, but their dress and fierceness sometimes scared colonists. A drawing of an Iroquois by a Frenchman in 1787 captures this fierceness.

The Yankee forts that were intended to counter the British forces were Forty Fort, the strongest fortification; Wilkes-Barre Fort; a stockaded house called Jenkins Fort; the small Pittstown Fort; and Wintermoot Fort.

Wintermoot Fort was manned by the Wintermoot, Van Alstyne and Scovell families, who were loyal to the Crown. In the early morning hours of July 3, Helmut Wintermoot arranged for the Fort to be staffed by sympathetic guards, who readily turned it over to John Butler. Wintermoot then advised John Butler as to the relative strength and location of Yankee forces, and Butler sent a small force to Jenkins Fort, which immediately surrendered.

At ten o'clock in the morning on July 3, John Butler sent three men under a flag of truce down to the Wyoming Valley. In return for the surrender of all forts, supplies and Continental soldiers in the area, all non-combatants would be allowed to leave with their possessions, and all military would be allowed to leave without their arms or possessions.

With no idea of the size of the British force, the Yankees refused the demand for surrender. Later that day, with the sound of drumbeats for accompaniment, in marched the Scots-Irish Paxton Boys, led by Lazarus Stewart.

John Butler proceeded to burn down Wintermoot Fort, much to the dismay and anger of Helmut Wintermoot. John Butler then sent a small decoy force of Rangers and Haudenosaunee, led by the Seneca chief Tawannears, to

Iroquois allant a la Decouverte

Costumes de Différents Pays, "*Iroquois Allant a la Decouverté,*" *c. 1797.* L.F. Labrousse. Jacques Grasset de Saint-Sauveur. Hand-tinted engraving on paper. Sheet 10 ¼ x 8 in.; Composition: 8 ¼ x 5 5/8 in. *Los Angeles County Museum of Art, Costume Council Fund (M.83.190.374).*

lure the Yankees into a trap. The decoy force retreated gradually, using the burning of Wintermoot Fort, along with other houses and outbuildings the British had set aflame, as a false indication of retreat.

Continental scouts reported that the British force was apparently in retreat, but there was a motion to wait for reinforcements, as there had been reports that Simon Spaulding was on his way home with two full companies of soldiers and would arrive in two or three days.

The militia, in true New England style, held a town meeting to decide whether to wait for reinforcements or to attack. Lazarus Stewart passionately argued for an attack, probably supported by the young and brash Wild Yankees who had followed his bloody lead over the past few years in ousting the Pennamite settlers.

At this point, wrote Eckert (1978), Stewart Lazarus may have said to Colonel Nathan Denison, who was allegedly a friend as well as a superior, "You're a damned coward! By God, I've a mind to report you to headquarters as being unfit to hold the rank you've got!"[67] Although Denison decried his friend's insubordination, Stewart's strident demands to begin the fight without waiting for reinforcements prevailed.

Shortly thereafter, an army of about 375 men and boys, trailed by applauding women and children, marched out of Forty Fort to the sound of the Irish tune "St. Patrick's Day in the Morning." They carried the new national flag, the stars and stripes.

The Yankee force paraded in line toward Wintermoot Fort, with braves helpfully retreating ahead of them. They marched in odd and even lines; every five paces one fired, while the other knelt to reload. Haudenosaunee braves and British Rangers periodically jumped out of the woods, fired and retreated, leading to (misguided) jubilance among the Yankees.

Soon the Yankees reached the remains of Wintermoot Fort, which was surrounded by a grassy plain with no cover. At the command of Colonel John Butler, in English and Seneca, the whole British force fired on the Continental soldiers. They were encircled by the Iroquois on their rear to prevent a retreat, and the slaughter began. Losses among the British and Haudenosaunee were reported to be about eleven, only two of whom were Rangers. Of the approximately four hundred Continental men, at least three hundred were killed and many more wounded. Among those who lost their lives were Lazarus Stewart and his son, Lazarus Jr.

The Battle of Wyoming took about a half hour, but according to later reports, destruction and terror continued for another eleven hours. The Articles of Capitulation between the British and the Americans signed

Massacre at Wyoming—Butler's Raid July 3 to July 4, 1778. Alonzo Chappel, artist. 1858. *Collection of Stephen B. Killian, Esq.*

on July 4, 1778, allowed the settlers to stay in their homes as long as they laid down their arms. As soon as the British left the valley, however, the Connecticut settlers were threatened and their homes plundered. Many fled, and many drowned in the Great Swamp or were lost in the wilderness.

General John Butler reported that he lost control of the Haudenosaunee, who destroyed buildings and plundered livestock. "But," reported the British general, "what gives me the sincerest satisfaction is that I can with great truth assure you that in the destruction of this settlement not a single person has been hurt of the Inhabitants, but such as were in arms, to those indeed the Indians gave no Quarter."[68]

The Americans who survived told tales of destruction and carnage. Queen Esther Montour, for example, was widely condemned for her supposed conduct. Esther was the granddaughter of the Seneca clan mother Kithinay and a Frenchman named Montour. Kithinay's daughter Margaret became known as "French Margaret" and established a Seneca village across from Tioga. French Margaret had two daughters; Catharine established a settlement at the head of Seneca Lake called Catharine's Town; Esther took over her mother's town when her mother died of smallpox and it became

Escape from the Wyoming Massacre. J. Steeple Davis, artist. 1896. *Collection of Stephen B. Killian, Esq.*

Queen Esther's Town. Because of her regal bearing, she was given the title Queen Esther. Esther's only child, Gencho, joined John Butler's forces against the Yankees in the Wyoming Valley, and on July 1, 1778, a few days before the Wyoming battle, Gencho was killed by a Yankee and his body badly mutilated.

Stories about Queen Esther's part in the battle were gleefully recounted by settlers of the valley for generations. According to reports gathered by Eckert, Esther Montour danced around a large rock in the firelight and bashed in the heads of captives arranged along the edge of the rock.

> *At the midpoint of this rock stood Queen Esther, clad only in a loincloth. In her hands she held a huge war club shaped like a bird's beak at the outermost end, with a rock firmly embedded in this opening…Her face and bare upper body were garishly painted with fearsome-looking sworls and lines of alternating black and white. Large, dead-white circles had been painted around her eyes and the eyes themselves were like black holes in a sort of living skull. She was a terrifying apparition. For nearly an hour Queen Esther had murmured and wailed and implored, jerking her body spastically atop the rock and reaching her hands upward in the darkness, beseeching powerful spirits to be with her, imploring them to make what was to come now a fitting retribution for the death of her only son, Gencho. Abruptly she signaled toward the warriors and several moved to the circle of captives and brought one of them to the front center of the rock and made him sit with his back against it. Then Queen Esther stepped forward and gripped the prisoner by the hair, jerked his head until the back of it was against the rock surface and the terrified eyes were staring straight upward into the night. Then, with a scream of the word "Gencho!" she brought the war club down on the forehead with all her strength, crushing the skull as if it were no more than an eggshell.*[69]

"The Bloody Rock" is now celebrated with an official Pennsylvania marker planted next to a small, fenced-in rock near the site of the Wyoming Battle.

Lebeus (Lebens) Hammond escaped from Queen Esther's slaughter, writes Eckert, by kicking and breaking free from his captors, running to the river and then to the marsh and hiding under a bush for two hours, then swimming downriver.

Queen Esther Inciting the Indians to Attack the Settlers at Wyoming. Joseph Brant and Colonel John Butler are seated on Esther's left. Howard Pyle, artist. *Scribner's Magazine,* April 1902.

The Bloody Rock where Queen Esther was alleged to have murdered several colonial soldiers. *Photograph by Stan Fox.*

The following story was told by Hammond about the behavior of Esther the day after the battle:

> Queen Esther was as prominent here as she had been in the slaughter of the night before. Col. Franklin relates that as he marched out with Col. Denison to introduce the victors through the gate of the fort, "Queen Esther, with all the impudence of an infernal being, turned to Col. Denison, and says, 'Well, Col. Den-ni-son, you make me promise to bring more Indians. Here, see (turning her hand back), I bring all these.' Col. J. Butler observed to her that women should be seen and not heard." Later in the day she was seen riding astride a stolen horse, on a stolen side-saddle placed with the hind end forward, with seven bonnets one upon the other on her head, with all the clothing she could contrive to get on, and over all a scarlet riding cloak, stolen from Mrs. Shoemaker, carrying in her hand a string of scalps freshly taken from the slaughtered friends of those who were the witnesses of her savage pride and the sufferers from her brutality.[70]

Atrocities by Tory soldiers were also reported, with Tory and Yankee brothers and former friends attacking and killing each other. Allan W. Eckert's 1978 narrative, from *The Wilderness War*, includes the following tale:

Lieutenant Elijah Shoemaker, his rifle lost, fled toward the river and plunged in. Some Indians and Tories who had been pursuing him stopped on the shoreline. Shoemaker could not swim well and knew he probably couldn't make it across. He stopped in water chest deep, afraid to go farther, yet determined to try if pursuit continued. Then he was amazed to hear someone on shore calling his name. He looked more closely and saw that one of the men who had been following him, even though hard to recognize because of the war paint on his face, was Henry Windecker. The Tory had previously worked for Shoemaker here in the Wyoming Valley and Shoemaker had done many favors for him. "Come on back to shore, Elijah," Windecker said, "You know you can't make it across. You'll drown. You'll be safe with me. Come on." Shoemaker hesitated…but the fear of drowning was strong and so finally he waded back and accepted Windecker's outstretched hand. Windecker began pulling him and then, with his free hand, suddenly jerked a tomahawk from his belt and drove it deep into the back of Shoemaker's head, killing him. He scalped the lieutenant and then shoved the body out into the current.[71]

Stephen B. Killian, Esquire, is a descendant of Elisha Richards, a patriot who died in the battle. He has collected stories and illustrations about the battle, which include the following narratives.[72]

Killian reports that Captain James Bidlack was captured and thrown alive onto the burning logs of Fort Wintermoot, where he was held down with a pitchfork until he died. Bidlack left a wife and several children. John Franklin, whose wife had died of smallpox, later married Mrs. Bidlack and helped to raise her children.

Another story is that Rufus Bennet was fleeing toward Forty Fort holding on to the tail of Colonel Butler's horse when, as he reached the stone bridge, he was about to be overtaken by pursuing Iroquois. Seeing Richard Inman lying on the ground, some say just awakening from the effects of consuming too much fortitude while the militia was in line at the creek earlier, Bennet called out if Inman's gun was loaded, and getting a reply that it was, asked Inman to shoot the pursuers. Inman dropped the lead "savage," and the others fled.

Killian also reports that Captain Ransom's body was found decapitated after the battle. Stories are told of fratricide, with rebel and Tory brothers involved in deadly exchanges. Giles Slocum reported that while he was hiding in Monockonock Island, he saw Henry Pencil reach the island and hide in the underbrush. Seeing his Tory brother John, he immediately threw

Escape of Rufus Bennet. Lossing & Barritt, engravers. 1858. *Collection of Stephen B. Killian, Esq.*

himself at his feet and begged for protection: "Save my life, brother and I will go with you and serve you as long as I live, if you will spare my life." John loaded his gun. Henry cried, "You won't kill your brother, will you?" John replied, "I will as soon as look at you. You are a damned rebel." He shot Henry, tomahawked and scalped him.

John's act was generally condemned. He ended up in Ontario with other Tories after the Revolution, and the story is told that he was attacked by wolves and the local Natives rescued him. He was attacked by wolves a second time, and the Natives saved him again. When the wolves attacked a third time, the Natives decided that this was his intended fate for killing his brother. They did not intervene, and the wolves killed John.[73]

After the battle, the Wyoming settlers fled, while the Iroquois and their allies, the British, were accused of plundering homes and possessions before riding off.

Early historians of the Haudenosaunee present a different view of the battle. Based on extensive interviews in the late nineteenth and early twentieth centuries, these White and Native historians express incredulity about the lurid stories told around the Battle of Wyoming: "Whites have always been prone to label any overwhelming Indian victory a massacre and to call any of their own battle triumphs over Indians a great victory," writes Graymont. About the story of Queen Esther, she writes, "All this is

The Fratricide at Wyoming. James Charles Armytage, engraver; Henry Warren, artist. 1860. *Collection of Stephen B. Killian, Esq.*

completely fictional, no women were along on the expedition, and no such sanguinary tortures took place."[74]

> *Although there was neither massacre nor torture of prisoners, the fleeing survivors spread lurid tales of atrocities; indeed, Wyoming became a symbol of Indian rapacity. Queen Esther…was reputed to have tomahawked helpless prisoners with her own hand; the "monster Brant" (who was not even at Wyoming, being occupied with the relatively bloodless raids on the Mohawk Valley at the time) was accused of murder; tales of the slaughter of whole families by their black-sheep Tory sons made frontier blood run cold.*[75]

A story of the Budd family by survivor Rachel Budd portrays a less brutal battle and aftermath than described by many historians. While living in Wyalusing, Rachel's husband, Benjamin, probably the father of kidnapper Frederick Budd, befriended Old Hendrick, assumed to be the Mohawk Peter Hendrick. Hendrick knew the Budd family in Wyalusing. When the fight began, the Budd family took refuge in Forty Fort, where Hendrick found them after the battle. He inquired about their two older sons, who were on their way to fight, and helped paint the family members' faces with vermilion for their protection. Later he led them through the battlefield and presented their two sons, also painted in vermilion, to them. Hendrick gave them horses and told them to go in peace, with his blessing.

Another story is told of Mrs. William (Elizabeth) Miller, who was taken prisoner at the battle with her child. After wandering about for a time, the braves decided to escort her back to her original home in Orange County, New York, and painted the faces of her and her child red "to show that

The Indians Departing After the Massacre of Wyoming. F.C. Yohn, artist. 1902–5. *Collection of Stephen B. Killian, Esq.*

they had been released that other Indians might not molest them." She was later reunited with her husband, who had been fighting elsewhere in the Continental army when the Battle of Wyoming occurred.[76]

Eckert's assertion that many captives were burned in the embers of a smoldering fort contrasts with Wallace's statement that, at the end of the battle, "the Seneca returned to Niagara with fifteen prisoners, whom they surrendered to the British; they received each a suit of clothes and some money, and went home, unaware that the military success of their mission was earning them an undeserved reputation for wanton savagery."[77]

Amanda C. Fontenova, director of library and archives, Luzerne County Historical Society, elucidates the discrepancy in narratives about the Battle of Wyoming and the behavior of Queen Esther:

> *It is very hard for modern-day historians to say we know exactly what went on during or after the battle when it comes to accounts of Queen Esther or "Indian savagery"; the primary source accounts that survive to this day, on either side, cannot be looked at as undiluted by emotions of some kind. Details may have been embellished upon or left out entirely to suit the teller of the tale, and to justify accusations, attacks, or retaliations in the aftermath.*

> *Trying to get an accurate list of the dead is another logistical nightmare, since it was weeks to months before any colonists came back to the valley to see what was left of their settlement, or even bury the dead. These were summer months, so identification of the bodies was not always easy. The men, women, and children who were not killed outright during the battle, fled the valley in all directions; even those who surrendered at the Fort were made to vacate the valley on foot. Some did not survive their flight through the wilderness, others simply never returned to the homes they started here.*[78]

Although there was initially no response by the Continental assembly and General Washington to the Battle of Wyoming, "the humiliating defeat at Wyoming, inflated in retrospect by atrocity stories, and the raids on frontier settlements in the Mohawk Valley were now beginning to spur action."[79]

Two hundred Continental militia under Colonels Hartley and Denison followed the Susquehanna up from the Wyoming Valley and burned three villages, including Queen Esther's Town. The Seneca, incensed by the exaggerated stories that were told of supposed Iroquois savagery at the Battle of Wyoming, continued their depredations.

In the following months, the British, Tory and Haudenosaunee forces undertook several attacks on settlers in New York and Pennsylvania, and in November 1778 Joseph Brant led an attack on Cherry Valley with 300 Tories and 152 Iroquois. The British leader had no control over the predations of his troops or the Native warriors. According to later accounts several prisoners were tortured, some cruelly, and many settlers were killed. Unlike the situation at Wyoming, writes Graymont, during this battle:

> *The Indians ranged throughout the settlement, plundering, burning, and killing. They just as readily dispatched the king's friends with the rebels. A number of Indian women were in the rear lines, armed with tomahawks for protection, watching for a safe moment to go pillaging. Some of the white soldiers were as active as the Indians in plundering. The Seneca warrior Blacksnake took no plunder on this expedition because, as he later explained, he thought it was bad enough to kill men and destroy their village.*[80]

Having been unjustly accused of barbarity, it was as though they felt a need to retaliate with barbarity.

Following the bloody Cherry Valley battle, British and Iroquois warriors continued their predations on the settlements in New York and Pennsylvania. The same warriors were involved in many of these battles, and Joseph Brant was often their leader. These incursions were ongoing as preparations were being made for a major campaign to destroy the Haudenosaunee.

Chapter 8

SULLIVAN'S CAMPAIGN

As stories about the Wyoming Massacre spread through the colonies, demands for retribution reverberated through the nascent Congress. The newly formed country vowed to punish the powerful Iroquois for their support of the British, while finally ending their attacks on frontier families. The solution was to be a destructive march across the lands occupied by the Haudenosaunee.

The soldiers of the Continental army were exhausted, underpaid and underfed, and so the initiative to create a powerful force capable of marching long distances and inflicting maximum damage took almost a year. There was also some disagreement as to whether such a punishment was needed or deserved.

The Quakers had argued for peace but were ignored. In addition, some Pennsylvanians were offended that the campaign would be led by a New Englander rather than a son of Pennsylvania. Furthermore, many Pennamites felt the destruction of the Yankee community at the Wyoming Massacre had been richly deserved. Having tried for decades to get rid of the Connecticut settlement, they had little desire to punish those who had done it for them.

Nevertheless, on February 25, 1779, Congress directed that the commander in chief take action for the "protection of the inhabitants and chastisement of the savages"[81] on the western frontiers. Volunteer soldiers were to be paid a bounty of one hundred dollars, as well as receiving pay and rations as soldiers in the Continental army.

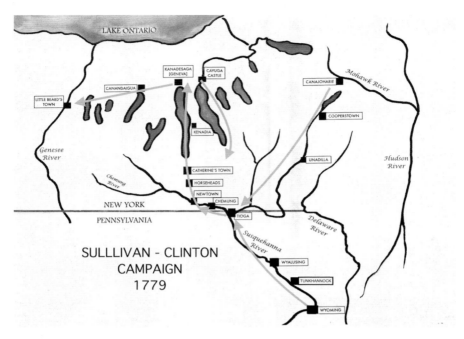

Above: Map of the Sullivan-Clinton Campaign against the Iroquois. *Drawing by Kathleen A. Earle.*

Opposite: *Major General John Sullivan.* Anonymous, British. August 22, 1776. *Metropolitan Museum of Art.*

The expedition consisted of two detachments: one would begin in Pennsylvania and follow the Susquehanna River to Geneva, New York; the other was to begin in the eastern part of New York and continue across New York, through the Mohawk country, meeting up with the first detachment along the way. Major General John Sullivan was ordered to assemble eleven continental regiments, approximately 2,500 men, at Easton, Pennsylvania, and march to Wyoming and from there up the Susquehanna. Meanwhile, five regiments under Brigadier General James Clinton would gather at Otsego Lake and float 1,500 men on twenty-two flatboats down the Unadilla River, by breaking a dam at the mouth of the lake. Colonel Daniel Broadhead was to lead a smaller force from Fort Pitt, Pennsylvania, up the Allegheny River.

Sullivan was Washington's second choice; his first choice, General Horatio Gates, had responded to Washington's appointment with regret, stating that he was "unequal" to the task given him by His Excellency, General Washington, and stating that he would forward the letter to General Sullivan as requested.[82]

John Sullivan was born in 1740 in Somersworth, New Hampshire. His father was an Irish immigrant who settled in Massachusetts around 1723. When the Revolution began, Sullivan was practicing law in New Hampshire. He was appointed brigadier general in 1775 and was promoted to major general as commander of forces in Canada in 1776. In the following years of the war, he led expeditions in Long Island, Staten Island, Brandywine and Germantown and was placed in charge of Rhode Island troops in 1778.

Sullivan's expedition was supposed to start in May. A letter from George Washington dated May 3, 1779, provided the following instructions:

> *Sir:—The expedition you are appointed to command is to be directed against the hostile tribes of the Six Nations of Indians, with their associates and adherents. The immediate object is their* total destruction and devastation, and the capture of as many persons of every age and sex as possible. It will be essential to ruin their crops now in the ground and prevent their planting more.[83]

The Oneida and Tuscarora tribes of the Haudenosaunee, whose braves fought largely on the Continental side against the British, were to be spared.

The Haudenosaunee who fought Sullivan and his soldiers included many of those involved in battles of the Revolution. Sayenqueraghta, Joseph Brant and Cornplanter were the head war chiefs. Others included Seneca warriors Half Town, Little Beard, Farmer's Brother, Jack Berry, Little Billy and Red Jacket; the Cayuga leader Fish Carrier; and Chief Sagwarithra of the Tuscarora. A few Delaware, led by Hochhadunk, joined the British forces along the way.[84]

Among the Wyoming Valley settlers who took part in Sullivan's campaign were Captain John Franklin, Wyoming Militia; Captain Simon Spaulding, Wyoming Independent Company; and John Jenkins, who acted as scout.

Sullivan assembled his headquarters for the mission against the Iroquois on May 24, 1779, in Easton. He was bogged down in preparations until June, finally reaching the Wyoming Valley on June 23. The troops had to cut a road from Easton to Wilkes-Barre. Part of Route 115 in Pennsylvania is still called "Sullivan's Trail."

From Wyoming, Sullivan ordered large amounts of supplies for the planned assault. These included unheard-of requests, including such luxuries as eggs and tongues, fifes, letter paper, wafers, quills, bells and sealing wax.

At the urging of Pennsylvania, Sullivan was censured for some of his requests, and when the supplies were delivered, they included much that was inferior to what was expected. Half of the cows, for example, were too sick to travel and had to be destroyed.

On July 24, 1779, Sullivan's march finally got underway. Between one hundred and two hundred boats carried baggage and artillery, 1,400 pack horses carried supplies and provisions and over two hundred cattle were

Between Wyalusing and Newtychanning, cows fell off the cliffs. *Original painting by Kathleen A. Earle.*

herded along the route. This grand spectacle was meant to impress both the settlers and any Native scouts in the area, who could report back to the Haudenosaunee.

As the march began out of the Wyoming Valley, steep cliffs were scaled and rivers crossed. On August 3 they reached Tunkhannock, and two days later they reached Wyalusing. The soldiers continued on through the Great Swamp, across high cliffs and over deep gullies and ravines. On the way to the small Iroquois village of Newtychanning, they traversed a path about a foot wide, with a 180-foot drop on one side. Several pack horses and three cows fell off the cliff and died.

On August 9, the thirty well-built houses of Newtychanning were burned to the ground. From here, the troops travelled to Queen Esther's Castle,[85] which had been destroyed the year before.

After several days withstanding rain, flooded rivers and almost impassable forest, the army reached the confluence of the Tioga and Susquehanna Rivers, where they waited for General Clinton's forces to meet up with them. Meanwhile, Clinton floated and marched his 1,500 men from eastern New York to meet Sullivan at Tioga. On the way, he undertook the total destruction of the Onondaga village. Over fifty houses were burned, the cultivated fields were destroyed and the cattle were all killed. The Onondaga, seeing the army coming, left even their weapons behind as they fled.

As he passed through Oneida country, Clinton tried to recruit members of the Oneida, who had been friendly to the Americans, to join his army. This was an extreme departure from Continental army protocol, as the Americans condemned the British for enlisting members of the Iroquois in their army. The British sent a warning to the Oneida not to join the Continental forces, threatening them with the wrath of the British king, and they generally complied. A few Oneida joined the army as scouts.

Three days after the Sullivan and Clinton forces met, on August 22, Sullivan discharged thirteen pieces of cannon in celebration. The combined force of almost four thousand men, several hundred cattle, over one thousand pack horses and nine cannon began the march north.

When they reached the Seneca village of Chemung, they found that most of the people had fled, leaving about forty British and Seneca above the village. This small force was quickly defeated, although the Seneca killed and wounded some of Sullivan's men. This is where John Franklin received his shoulder wound. From Chemung, they went to Newtown.

Sullivan's progress from the beginning of the campaign to Little Beard's Town was described in diaries by soldiers who marched with him. Some of these were collected in 1887 by Frederick Cook in *Journals of the Military Expedition of Major General John Sullivan against the Six Nations of Indians in 1779.* Cook was secretary of state for New York at the time. The following excerpts from these diaries bring the march to life.

The men whose diary entries follow are:

LIEUTENANT JOHN JENKINS: Jenkins was a guide for the campaign.

LIEUTENANT COLONEL ADAM HUBLEY: Hubley was commissioned as first lieutenant in the First Pennsylvania Battalion in 1775 and promoted to lieutenant colonel in 1777. He led the Eleventh Pennsylvania Regiment on Sullivan's march.

SERGEANT THOMAS ROBERTS: Roberts was a shoemaker by trade and a resident of Middletown Point (now Matawan), New Jersey. He attained the rank of sergeant in the Fifth New Jersey Regiment.

MAJOR JOHN BURROWES: Burrowes was a merchant from Middletown Point. Under General David Forman, nicknamed Black David, he was named by the Tories "Black David's Devil." With Rogers, he was a member of the Fifth New Jersey Regiment.

> *Aug. 5th* [Jenkins]*: The army marched about 10 o'clock and encamped at night at Wyalusing. I left a bay mare at Van der Lypp's, on account of her being lame and not able to go further. One of the men…was unwell and was left in the encampment. One of the boat men fell out of the boat and was unfortunately drowned.*

> *Aug. 5th* [Hubley]*: This valley was formerly called Oldman's Farm, occupied by the Indians and white people; together they had about sixty houses, a considerable Moravian meeting house, and sundry other public buildings; but since the commencement of the present war the whole has been consumed and laid waste, partly by the savages and partly by our own people. The land is extraordinarily calculated chiefly for meadows. The grass at this time is almost beyond description, high and thick, chiefly blue grass, and the soil of the land very rich. The valley contains about 1200 acres of land, bounded on one side by an almost inaccessible mountain and on the other by the river Susquehanna.*

Aug. 9th [Jenkins]: This day in passing a narrow defile in break-neck hill, three of our oxen fell off and were killed. At night one of the small boats loaded with flour was stove, and the lading lost.

Aug. 13th [Jenkins]: The party arrived at Chemung about 5 o'clock, in the morning, but found that the enemy had left the town. We followed them about one mile, and as our advance party, under the command of Gen. Hand was ascending a small hill, the enemy fired upon them from the top. After a spirited contest, the enemy fled taking with them their dead and wounded. We had three brave officers,—Capt. Henry Carberry, Capt. John Franklin and Lieut. William Huston wounded, together with a number of men—and six men killed. After gaining the summit of the hill, we halted for some time and then returned to the town, and set it on fire, and destroyed fifteen acres of corn.

Aug. 17th [Jenkins]: The party marched at six o'clock in the morning and encamped at night on Owego Flats near the river, where there was an Indian town. The Indians had left the town, however, some time before our arrival.

On August 23 John Jenkins reported that he delivered shoes to twenty-one soldiers, including John Swift, who would later accompany him to New York State to survey the Phelps and Gorham Purchase.

Up until this point, the Sullivan and Clinton armies had met limited resistance. But at Newtown, now Elmira, New York, scouts reported that a large Iroquois and British force was prepared to meet Sullivan's army. On August 29, Sullivan began his attack on Newtown. The British and the Haudenosaunee fought bravely but were overpowered by the much greater Continental force. As was their choice when involved in a losing battle, the Iroquois began to leave, signaling their intent to their comrades with a peculiar yell used for that purpose. After six hours, the conflict was over. Jenkins wrote in his diary:

Aug. 29th [Jenkins]: Soon after our cannon began to play upon them, they ran off and left their breastworks, in the most precipitous manner, leaving their packs, blankets, tomahawks, spears, etc. behind them. At the same time we took possession of the enemy's ground and fortifications.

Captured prisoners from the battle at Newtown told the Continentals that there had been five hundred Iroquois and two hundred Tories in the battle, and when the Iroquois retreated, so did the British. According to Graymont (1972), Red Jacket was the first to leave the battle, and the others followed.

From Newtown, Sullivan's troops had several days in which they did not meet any resistance. The Iroquois were badly disheartened and left their villages to be overrun and destroyed by the enemy. Except for long days of marching, the battles consisted primarily of burning crops and houses, with the occasional capture of an Iroquois brave. The diary of Sergeant Thomas Roberts contains this incident:

> *Aug. 30th* [Roberts]*: This morning some of our Trupes Went in the Woods Sirching for plunder and found 4 Indians and Sculpd them and Brought them Into Camp one was one of the Cheafs Besides a Grate deel of other phlnder of all Kinds.*

Barbara Graymont, in *The Iroquois in the American Revolution.* (1972) reports that on August 30, half of Sullivan's army was out cutting down corn, which had grown to about sixteen feet high. She states:

> *It is the business of a soldier to know how to kill, but the business of this campaign would prove a strange task indeed for men at arms—a warfare against vegetables.*[86]

The following incident was related in two of the diaries:

> *Aug. 31st* [Roberts]*: This morning Our trupes found 2 Indians and Skin thear Legs & Drest them for Leggins.*[87]

At the end of August, fifty of Sullivan's horses could go no further, and he ordered the horses shot. Later, the horses' heads were arranged beside the trail, and the town was named Horseheads. The army continued north and on September 1 reached Catharine's Town at about seven o'clock, only to find that it had been evacuated. This was the town that was named after Catharine Montour, sister to Queen Esther. Hubley described the town:

> *Sept. 2nd* [Hubley]*: Catharines town is pleasantly situated on a creek, about three miles from Seneca lake; it contained nearly fifty houses, in general, very good—the country near is very excellent. We found several very fine corn-fields, which afforded the greatest plenty of corn, beans,*

etc., of which, after our fatiguing march, we had an agreeable repast.... The lands are rich, abounding with fine, large, and clear timber, chiefly white oak, hickory, walnut and ash; bounded on the left for about three miles with excellent marsh or meadow ground, after which proceeds the beautiful Seneca lake, which abounds with all kinds of fish, particularly salmon, trout, rock, that which resembles perch, as also sheep-head....It is about three miles in breadth, and about forty miles in length. Upon the right, though considerably up the country, is another delightful lake, called Kayuga lake; abounds with all kinds of fish also, and is about forty miles in length. We proceeded along this beautiful country about twelve miles, and encamped near a corn-field, on which stood several Indian cabins.... Previous to our arrival here the Indians who occupied the cabins already mentioned, probably discovered our approach, pushed off precipitously, leaving their kettles with corn boiling over the fire.

Sept. 5th: About 9 o'clock this morning the army moved through a country much the same as yesterday. About 12 o'clock we arrived at Canadia, about three miles from the last encampment, where we encamped for this night.... An Indian, who lay concealed, fired, but without effect on our rifleman and immediately fled. [A freed Indian prisoner] *informed us that Brant, with near a thousand savages, including Butler's Rangers, left this town last Friday, seemingly much frightened and fatigued—that they were pushing for Kanadaugua, an Indian village, where they mean to make a stand and give us battle....Canadia is much the finest village we have yet come to. It is situated on a rising ground, in the midst of an extensive apple and peach orchard, within half a mile of Seneca lake; it contains about forty well-finished houses, and everything about it seems neat and well improved.*

Today the town of Catharine is a small hamlet located in the area of Catharine's Town. An Episcopal church founded in 1810 still serves the area.

Sullivan's troops marched across the bountiful, lush valleys of upstate New York, encountering many surprises along the way. Fruits and vegetables, carefully grown and tended by the Iroquois, were eagerly wolfed down by Sullivan's troops, who were amazed at the huge orchards and unending fields of corn, squash, beans, tobacco and vegetables cultivated by the supposed savages. Houses were well made and furnished, and barns housed cattle, pigs and horses.

And there were also, here and there, white faces. These were the captives who had been taken over many years, some now left in the villages by the

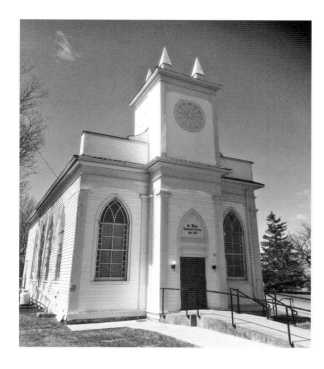

Episcopal Church in Catharine, New York, established 1810 at the site of Catharine's Town. *Photograph by Stan Fox.*

retreating villagers. One small boy was described in the diary of Major John Burrows:

> *Sept. 7* [Burrowes]: *We found a little white child about four or five years old. He can understand English and talked Indian. He is very poor and appears to have been sick. When he was found he was entirely naked. The officer that has him, has got clothes for him which seems to please the little fellow much.*

Many adoptees were gathered up by Sullivan's forces and taken back to their original colonial communities.

Only one more skirmish met Sullivan's forces. On September 13 near the town of Genesee, also known as Little Beard's Town, some of Sullivan's men were killed by Haudenosaunee and British warriors who were lying in wait for the main force, and their bodies were left in pieces for the army to find. Among the bodies was that of the Continental army Oneida scout Lieutenant Thaosagwat. His elder brother was fighting with the British, and although he berated his younger brother for helping the rebels, he could not kill him.

Mary Jamison reported the encounter of the two Oneida brothers to an interviewer in 1824. Aware that Sullivan's army was approaching, the women were sent into the woods, she reported, while the braves lay in wait for the army. When Thaosagwat was captured, his brother said to him:

> *Brother! You have merited death; and shall have your desserts! When the rebels raised their hatchets to fight their good master, you sharpened your knife, you brightened your rifle, and led on our foes to the fields of our fathers!…When those rebels had driven us from the fields of our fathers to seek out new homes, it was you who could dare to step forth as their pilot, and conduct them even to the doors of our wigwams, to butcher our children, and to put us to death! No crime can be greater! But though you have merited death and shall die on this spot, my hands shall not be stained in the blood of a brother!* Who will strike? [88]

And then Little Beard struck Thaosagwat dead. The other Oneida ran away, and in pursuing him the warriors came across another small detachment of Sullivan's men, killed all but two and brought those back to be brutally tortured. Haudenosaunee involved in this encounter included Sayenqueraghta, Joseph Brant, Sagwarithra, Cornplanter, Little Beard, Fish Carrier and Blacksnake.

Although there were few casualties on either side, Sullivan destroyed all the Haudenosaunee towns on the Susquehanna River and almost all of the main settlements of the Cayuga and Seneca. Killian reports, "To prove the effectiveness of the Sullivan expedition's mission to make the Iroquois' country uninhabitable for years to come and rendering the Iroquois totally dependent on the British, General Sullivan, in his report to the President and congress stated, 'We have not left a single settlement or field of corn in the country of the Five Nations.'" [89]

The destruction of Iroquois country earned Washington the Haudenosaunee moniker "Town Destroyer," or "Destroyer of Villages," a title that has been applied ever since to the president of the United States.

Many Iroquois relocated to Canada, where a large contingent of the Six Nations lives today at Grand River, located between Hamilton, Brantford and Simcoe, Ontario. Members of the Mohawk, Oneida, Onondaga, Cayuga, Seneca and Tuscarora live on small reservation lands in New York State; the Cayuga live with the Seneca. The Haudenosaunee continue to be outraged by Sullivan's destruction of their original homeland.

When the United States Constitution was adopted, Indian Nations were described as sovereign, and Native affairs were considered to be within the responsibility of the federal rather than the state governments.[90] This designation gives the 574 federally recognized tribes in the United States the same autonomy as states and does not allow the states to oversee their affairs.

Chapter 9

THE YANKEE-PENNAMITE

WARS CONTINUE

Haudenosaunee attacks continued sporadically over the next few years but were not as devastating. Sullivan's campaign against the Iroquois, however, had no effect on the battles that were ongoing between the Connecticut Yankees and the Pennamites. Although the Pennamites objected strenuously, people trying to escape the crowded towns of New England continued to pour into the Wyoming Valley. And no wonder; nourished by the Susquehanna River and its tributaries, the valley was described as mountainous but picturesque, lush and fertile, nourished by the river running though the valley below.[91]

Through fits and starts, both Pennamite and Yankee settlers battled for the land given their forebears by King Charles. The Connecticut Yankees controlled the valley from about 1770, and in 1775 Connecticut created a separate county in the Wyoming Valley called Westmoreland. But still tensions ran high between Yankees and Pennamites.

Benjamin Bidlack was one of many Yankees caught up in the conflict. He was arrested by Pennamites in Sunbury while on a commercial venture and was imprisoned in a makeshift jail. He soon befriended his captors, as he was "a splendid singer and a merry fellow…addicted to strong drink."[92] Over time, he convinced his jailers that he could best lead them in song if he was outside the jail, on the front stoop. One night he introduced a new song, "The Old Swaggering Man," accompanied by merrymaking and hard drink. As he reached the chorus, Bidlack jumped from the stoop, scaled the six-foot fence around the jail and headed off into the woods. Many of his

Bidlack's Escape. Lossing & Barritt, engravers, 1858. *Collection of Stephen B. Killian, Esq.*

listeners roared with laughter, while some tried to chase him. He traveled fifty miles back to his home in Plymouth, Wyoming Valley.

In 1782, three years after the rout of the Iroquois by Sullivan's campaign, the Connecticut settlers suffered a major setback when a newly formed national court in Trenton, New Jersey, ruled that land claimed by Connecticut belonged to Pennsylvania. The Trenton Decree was based partly on the premise that, since the Iroquois were technically landless nomads, they were not able to sell any land, and the sale of the Wyoming Valley land in 1754 was therefore invalid. This decision also signaled the waning influence and importance of the Haudenosaunee in the affairs of the European settlers.

After the Trenton Decree, the state favored Pennamite settlers and wealthy Pennsylvania land investors over Yankee land claimants, in both correspondence and action. But the Yankees, convinced of their right to the land, continued to fight, rushing out of the woods, sometimes in feathers and blackface, to attack their Pennsylvania neighbors. New Yankee settlers continued to purchase shares from the Susquehannah Company and to relocate to the Wyoming Valley.

In July 1785 the Susquehannah Company offered three hundred acres free to any man who would immediately settle on the land, defend the Connecticut claim and remain for three years. Three hundred acres was half the size of a standard share of six hundred acres; the men who accepted this agreement, along with others who had bought half shares earlier, were known as half-share men. In 1785, the half-share men were told that if they did not occupy the land by October 1, 1786, the company would revoke their ownership. Connecticut settlers already living in the Valley also took advantage of this deal. Several of the kidnappers, or members of their families, whether new to the area or longtime residents, became new half-share men.

Meanwhile, war between the Connecticut and the Pennsylvania settlers continued to fester and boil, as both Pennamites and Yankees attacked each other's homes and livestock.

In January 1787, Timothy Pickering moved from Philadelphia to Wilkes-Barre in the Wyoming Valley to investigate and quell the Yankee rebellion. That year was notable for an escalation of tensions between the Connecticut and Pennsylvania claimants.

Pickering initially met with a variety of local people and called for new local elections. In February, John Franklin was elected by a great majority as Luzerne County representative to the Pennsylvania General Assembly. Pickering immediately questioned Franklin's motives for running, believing him to be acting against the best interests of Pennsylvania.

At Pickering's request, on March 28, 1787, Pennsylvania passed the Confirming Act, which recognized the tenure of Connecticut claimants who had settled the land before the Trenton Decree of 1782. This left out those settlers who had obtained land since 1782; notably, it ignored many of the half-share men.

This act split the Yankee sympathies between old and new Connecticut settlers. The Pennsylvania settlers objected to the act as well, as it legitimized some of the Connecticut landholdings. It was later repealed, but not until April 1, 1790.

In May 1787, eighty Yankees signed a petition that consolidated opposition to Pennsylvania and named John Franklin as leader of the Connecticut claimants. Two weeks later, the Susquehannah Company reinforced this initiative by appointing John Franklin as their agent.[93]

The following story involving Yankee settler Zebulon Marcy, written by his descendant Hatsy Eberhardt in 1976, illustrates the complicated relationships among Wyoming Valley settlers.

Marcy, born in 1744 in Dover, Dutchess County, New York, was one of the earliest settlers to move to the Wyoming Valley under the auspices of the Susquehannah Company. The trail to the bottomlands of the Susquehanna River was rough. Zebulon and his brother Ebenezer were among the hardy pioneers who traveled south along the Delaware River, over the mountains and along the Lackawanna River to the valley. In 1770, the Marcy brothers built a log cabin where the Lackawanna spilled into the Susquehanna, near the present location of Pittstown. According to Eberhardt:

> *It had taken them two weeks to clear a single acre of land. As they cut the trees, they sorted out those of a suitable size for building the cabin; the rest were dragged into huge piles and burned. They had had to borrow a neighbor's oxen for that part of the job and for the planting the of the first wheat crop....A three-cornered plow which was hewn from a tree crotch and had wooden pins set in it at intervals, was drawn over the ground among the stumps....The cabin they'd constructed was about 15 foot square and about 7 feet high. It had an earthen floor and a bark roof. The fireplace was a backdrop and hearth of stones cemented in place with mud. A hole was left in the roof for the smoke to escape. The doors and windows were simply openings cut in the sides of the cabin.*[94]

Zebulon Marcy gradually improved his cabin, adding greased paper to cover the windows in 1771 and making furniture and a latch-string door. In 1772 he sold this rudimentary house to his brother and relocated to Tunkhannock. There he constructed a more substantial home, complete with apple trees, corn and wheat fields, in the flatlands of the Susquehanna.

Cottage similar to that built by Zebulon Marcy in the Wyoming Valley. *In Munsell*, History of Luzerne, Lackawanna and Wyoming Counties, PA, *1880.*

During the Revolution, Eberhardt writes, it was "supposedly" Marcy who killed Queen Esther's son Gencho, and during the Battle of Wyoming Zebulon was not to be found. Two weeks after the battle, his wife and children accompanied relatives back to Fishkill, New York, on a long and difficult journey through the wilderness. In 1785, Zebulon brought them back and built a new house in Tunkhannock.

When Pickering arrived, Marcy was one of the Connecticut settlers who favored an oath of allegiance to Pennsylvania. According to Eberhardt, he had been a staunch supporter of Franklin and the Yankees, but he was also a justice of the peace, and in that role he was given the responsibility of getting other Connecticut residents of Tunkhannock to sign the oath. This did not sit well with his Yankee friends and neighbors.

Around the time of the kidnapping in June 1788, an angry mob went to the house of Marcy in Tunkhannock, took off the roof and levelled the house. The attack on Marcy's house was an attack by the Connecticut Yankees on one of their own who did not follow the party line, regarded with suspicion as being on Pickering's side. During Pickering's kidnapping, some of the articles that Pickering sent for were delivered to and from Marcy's house, and when he was released, Pickering had his first meal at the Marcy home and stayed overnight.

In the fall of 1788, the Court of Quarter Sessions at Wilkes-Barre charged Zebulon Cady, Solomon Earl, Daniel Earl and Wilkes Jenkins with "riot and unlawful assembly and with pulling down the mansion house of Zebulon Marcy" in June. Stephen Jenkins was charged in the same court, with the "forcible entry of a lot of land in Tunkhannock, in the possession of Zebulon Marcy, and with assault and battery upon the person of Lydia Marcy."[95]

Marcy stayed in Tunkhannock, at one point challenging another resident to a duel. According to Eberhardt:

> *Zebulon Marcy was a straight, sturdy, well-built man with a bold, daring countenance. He was a tall and commanding presence and was known as a man of clear, positive convictions and possessed of the courage to assert them. He had an aggressive spirit and an indomitable will.*[96]

He died at his home in Tunkhannock in 1834 at age ninety-one.

Chapter 10

THE KIDNAPPERS

T he family background of the kidnappers is not easy to ascertain. More than two centuries after the event, records regarding the ancestry of the fifteen young men are sketchy or incomplete. Historical records that are available indicate that they were almost all descendants of the approximately twenty thousand English men, women and children who crossed the Atlantic between the landing of the Mayflower in 1620 and the English Civil War in 1640 as part of "the Great Migration." They had ties by kinship and association; some apparently were related or knew each other from their previous homes in Connecticut, Vermont, or New York. In the Wyoming Valley, they lived in towns that clustered around the Susquehanna River.

Conflicts engrained pugnacious behavior. During the Yankee-Pennamite wars, the kidnappers became inured to attacking their neighbors while wearing blackface and feathers; Pickering's abduction was an extension of the trouble they were already in. Their older relatives told them they would back them up with supplies and support, and the *great men* promised them land and money. Later, some reported they were threatened or ordered to take part. For example, according to the mother of two of the kidnappers, an elderly man in the Valley who claimed he was too old and blind to take part ordered his grandson to join the kidnappers and offered a gun and ammunition to another boy.

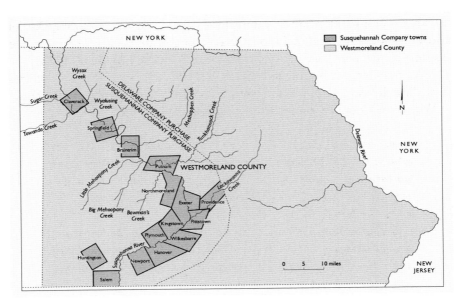

Map reprinted from *Wild Yankees: The Struggle for Independence along Pennsylvania's Revolutionary Frontier*, by Paul B. Moyer. *Copyright © 2007 by Cornell University. Included by permission of the publisher, Cornell University Press.*

Through the lens of 230 years, the Yankees appear to have been living in a mélange of misery and violence. Yet the family histories of the kidnappers portray their ancestors as farmers, shoemakers, blacksmiths, tailors and other respectable men, whose sons or grandsons should have prospered in their new homes along the Susquehanna.

ZEBULON CADY AND THE EARL BOYS

Members of the Cady and Earle[97] families lived in Pomfret, Windham County, Connecticut, and members of both the Cady and Earle/Earl families owned land in the Wyoming Valley before 1782.

They appear to have been neighbors and friends. Living in Tunkhannock in the 1780s, at least two Earl boys and Zebulon Cady were rowdy and enthusiastic Wild Yankees. In 1787, stalwart Obadiah Gore told Timothy Pickering that the half-share men "up the river are breathing out Threatenings, particularly…Solo & Dan Earle Jun make use of the most Blasphemous Expressions that I ever heard being Uttered from any person."[98] Pickering described Zebulon Cady in two different documents as "an atrocious villain" and "a notorious villain." As noted earlier, Daniel and Solomon Earl and Zebulon Cady, along with Wilkes Jenkins, were responsible for the attack on Zebulon Marcy's house in June of 1788.

Benjamin, who later turned state's witness, was not linked to stories regarding the behavior of Daniel and Solomon, except for the kidnapping.

Windham County, Connecticut, was organized in 1726. By that time:

> *Forests had been leveled, roads constructed, streams bridged, and land subdued and brought under cultivation. The aboriginal inhabitants were fast passing away. The wigwam was superseded by the farm house, and the tomahawk by the woodman's axe and plow. Several hundred families were now settled here, with comfortable prospects ahead....*
>
> *Among the men of the time there was much coarseness and roughness, much bickering and backbiting, but withal a high sense of personal dignity, which was easily offended by the tongue of slander. The first generation reared in these new towns was probably inferior in education and culture to the standard of their fathers. Schools, poor at best, were maintained with great difficulty, and books were scarce....The court records furnish abundant testimony to the roughness and violence of the times, and church records bear equal evidence to much looseness of morals among the people. With all their strictness in Sabbath keeping and catechizing, in family and church discipline, there was great license in speech and manner, much hard drinking and rude merry-making, with occasional outbreaks of border ruffianism.[99]*

A few hundred Wabbaquassets and Quinebaugs lived in the area, and Mohegans and Shetuckets roved through the towns.

The Earle and Cady families of Pomfret were among those settlers who came from England during the Great Migration.

The probable ancestor of Zebulon was Nicholas Cady, born in 1627 in Stoke-by-Nayland, Suffolk, England. Nicholas and his wife, Judith, immigrated to Watertown, Massachusetts, in 1645. The family moved from Watertown to Killingly (part of Pomfret), where Zebulon Cady was born in 1767.

The three Earl boys may have been descendants of Ralph Earle of Bishop's Stortford, County Herts, England, and his wife Joan, née Savage. Ralph and Joan set off in 1634 across the great sea and landed in what is now Rhode Island. Ralph and Joan's descendant William Earle married Hepzibah Butts of Killingly, near Pomfret. Their sons Nathaniel, John and William bought land in Pomfret in 1731, and then Nathaniel and John migrated to Beekman Patent, Dutchess County, New York. William stayed in Pomfret, from where his son Daniel Earle allegedly moved to the Susquehanna River area. Substantiation of Daniel's move to the Wyoming Valley is provided in a history of Kalamazoo, Michigan:

> *The Earl family was originally from Connecticut. Daniel Earl…was a near neighbor and friend of Gen. Israel Putnam, of Revolutionary memory; but little is now known about his history, except that he removed to Pennsylvania and settled on the Susquehanna River, where he remained for seven or eight years, when he removed to Ontario Co., N.Y., where he died at an advanced age. He was a farmer by occupation and reared a family of ten children. William Earl [son of Daniel] was born in Pennsylvania in 1782. Subsequently he removed to Yates County, N.Y.* [and then to Michigan].[100]

General Israel Putnam is credited by some as the soldier who said "Don't fire until you see the whites of their eyes" at the battle of Bunker Hill in the American Revolution. A resident of Pomfret, Putnam took part in the siege of Havana, Cuba, in which Daniel Earle's brother Moses was killed "in His Majesties Service" in 1762.[101]

Putnam, one of the original towns in the Wyoming Valley, was named after General Putnam. The name of the town was changed to Tunkhannock in 1786 and the boundaries enlarged.

William Earle was assigned a pew, in 1740, at the meetinghouse called the Second Church of Pomfret, serving the inhabitants of Pomfret, Canterbury and Mortlake (now Brooklyn). Members of the Cady family (Daniel, Ezekiel, Uriah and Jonathan) were also assigned pews. The replacement building for this church was built in 1771 under the leadership of Putnam, who was buried from that church "in what was called the most magnificent funeral that Windham County had ever seen."[102] This church became Connecticut's first Unitarian church in 1822. The building was recently restored to its original 1771 appearance.

In the Wyoming Valley, Daniel Earl was a Susquehannah Company proprietor who, with Jephthah Earl,[103] owned land before the Trenton Decree of 1782.

The *Remonstrance of Luzerne Inhabitants against William Montgomery*, on September 18, 1787, was signed by Daniel Earll, Daniel Earll Jr., Jephthah Earll, Solomon Earll, Benjamin Earll, and Joseph Earl.[104]

The Second Church of Pomfret in Mortlake, Connecticut.
Photograph by Stan Fox.

Although letters and statements from the Susquehannah Company papers frequently refer to Benjamin, Daniel and Solomon Earl as brothers, or as sons of Joseph, it is possible that one or more of these young men were sons of Daniel Earl of Pomfret. The grandson of William Earle (Sr.) and his wife Hepzibah, Daniel was living in Tunkhannock at the time of the kidnapping. Also, the kidnapper Daniel Earl was sometimes referred to as "Daniel Earl Jr."

Besides the elder Daniel's father, William, William and Hepzibah Earle of Pomfret had a son named Joseph Earle, born in 1702, who appears from genealogical records to have been in Pomfret and at the Beekman Patent in Dutchess County, New York. Joseph's son, also named Joseph, may have been the "Joseph Earl" who was said to be the father of one or more of the Earl boys who kidnapped Pickering. During his captivity, Pickering wrote that a "Joseph Earl" was the father of *two* of the Earl boys. It is also possible that there was another Earl/Earle who was father of one of the kidnappers, as the term "son" was frequently used to denote cousins in the Earle family at that time.

The Settlers of the Beekman Patent (1990–2003) records a Joseph Earl born about 1730 with sons Solomon, Daniel, William, John and Joseph and daughter Lois. There is no child named Benjamin listed. This Joseph Earl moved from the town of Nine Partners in the Beekman Patent to Danby, Vermont, and then to the Wyoming Valley. He was one of the first settlers of Danby. A short biographical sketch from Danby states that:

> *Earl, Joseph, from Nine Partners, in 1765, was the second settler in town…and seems to have been a man of ability and bore conspicuous part in organizing society. He also served the town in various ways but was not long a resident here. He left during the Revolutionary war, but we are not informed to what place he emigrated.*[105]

This Joseph Earl appears to have moved from Danby to Shoreham, Vermont. His home on Lake Champlain, recently restored, served as the staging area for Ethan Allen's attack on Fort Ticonderoga during the Revolution. Joseph's house was directly across from Fort Ticonderoga, on a "slight rise overlooking and commanding a view of the cove, at a distance of a few hundred yards."[106]

Joseph Earl's house looking across Lake Champlain to Ticonderoga. *Photograph by Stan Fox.*

Joseph and his wife, Phebe, sold their Vermont land in 1784. A year later, "Joseph Earl" is listed as a half-share man in the Wyoming Valley. It is possible that the Joseph Earl from Vermont moved to the Wyoming Valley at about the same time as Ethan Allen, whom he apparently knew.

To further complicate the genealogy of the Earl boys, there was another Earl family in Luzerne. Ebenezer Earl settled in Northampton County about 1764. Descendants of Ebenezer named James, Edward, Samuel and Ebenezer Jr. appear in Luzerne County records. The 1790 census for Luzerne lists James, Ebenezer and Samuel as residents, along with Benjamin, Joseph and Daniel Earl. An "Ebenezer Earl" appears to have been on both sides of the Yankee-Pennamite wars. Ebenezer Earl was part of a posse from Northumberland County, Pennsylvania, who went to Luzerne County on January 18, 1771, to dispossess the Connecticut "Rioters."[107] And James and Ebenezer Earl were reputedly among those chased from their homes by Pennamites in 1784.[108]

The three Earl kidnappers were doubtless unaware of, and probably disinterested in, their heritage. Their focus was on the time and place where they were living in 1788. About two weeks after the kidnapping, Zebulon Cady, Daniel Earl and Solomon Earl sent Pickering a letter:

> *To Cornel piCrien*
> *We humblely beg your Parden for what we have don and am determed to Inform Aginst Avry man that have brot us In the onhapy durty Afair but we hope that your will hav marcy on us for we humbley beg forgivness...*[109]

By this time Benjamin Earl had been captured. The letter requested that Pickering let Daniel and Solomon know what would be done with them and with Benjamin.

FREDERICK BUDD

Frederick Budd was among those who went to visit the *great men* during the kidnapping, while the other Boys guarded Pickering in the woods, indicating Budd was important or motivated enough to take a leadership role.

The most likely ancestor of Frederick was John Budd, who arrived in Boston in 1637–38 from Chichester, Sussex, England. Frederick's link to this family is supported by the fact that Benjamin Budd, great-grandson of John and probable father of Frederick, was an early shareholder in the

Susquehannah Company. He moved to Orange County from Long Island, New York, with his wife, Rachel, and then, around 1768, to Springfield, Wyoming Valley. In 1769, Benjamin and Rachel's son Susquehanna was the first non-Native child born in the valley. In 1774, Benjamin built a rough cabin on the Susquehanna River, across from Wyalusing, and was reported to be living there with his wife, six sons and two daughters. According to Clement Ferdinand Heverly's *History and Geography of Bradford County, PA, 1615–1924* (1926), Benjamin's three older sons John (b. 1750), Joseph (b. 1752) and Asa (b. 1757) fought in the Wyoming Massacre, while their father Benjamin, who was suspected of being a pacifist and/ or a Tory, did not. This story differs from that reported by Rachel Budd, alluded to above, to a French interviewer in 1787. Rachel stated that her two older sons were rescued while on the way to the battle by a friendly Mohawk, Old Hendrick, who painted the faces of the family members red, gave them horses and sent them on their way. Some sources report that Joseph Budd, who was killed in the Wyoming Battle, was one of Benjamin's sons.

Gideon and Joseph Dudley and Timothy Kilborn

The Dudley and Kilborn boys were supported and encouraged in the kidnapping plot by their fathers, Martin Dudley and Joseph Kilborn. In the "Deposition of Daniel Earll and Statement of Solomon Earll" on September 13, 1788, Daniel stated that

> *Martin Dudley…& Joseph Kilborn manifested great satisfaction for the same cause* [taking Colonel Pickering], *and furnished us with victuals with signs of pleasure and hearty good will, as persons would naturally do who were pleased with any measure which they were willing and desiring to support.*[110]

Kilborn's house was about a mile from where Pickering was held in the woods, and Joseph Kilborn provided wheat and bread to the kidnappers. He was overheard saying, the day before the kidnapping:

> *If Pickering & his laws are any thing, I am nothing, and hold no lands: but if I am any thing, & hold land, then Pickering & his laws are nothing; and we shall know in a few days how the matter will turn.*[111]

Timothy Kilborn was one of two, with Daniel Taylor, who put chains on Pickering after they had been in the woods for some time. After the kidnapping, Pickering referred to him as "Young Kilborn who had particularly insulted me."

Timothy's little brother Aaron, fifteen at the time of the kidnapping, appeared to run errands and carry messages for the group. Later, Pickering mentioned Aaron's young age at least twice. Timothy was twenty years old.

Captain Martin Dudley was Pickering's neighbor in Wilkes-Barre. Pickering recognized the Dudley boys during his kidnapping when the blackface wore off. The mother of Gideon and Joseph, Anna Dudley, did not want her sons to get involved, while Martin stated that he only wanted Gideon, and not Joseph, to join the kidnappers. Gideon Dudley was identified as one of the leaders. As mentioned previously, Gideon had wanted to handcuff Pickering when they were at Joseph Earl's house.

Both the Dudley and Kilborn families were from Litchfield County, Connecticut, and both settled in the Wyoming Valley before 1787. In Susquehannah Company papers in 1787, Joseph Kilborn was listed as a cordwainer[112] from Plymouth (next to Wilkes-Barre), and Martin Dudley was listed as a husbandman from "Wilkesborough."

The probable ancestor of Timothy and Aaron Kilborn was Thomas Kilbourne, born in Wood Ditton, England, in 1578, the descendant of Sir William de Kilbourne, Lord of the Manor of Kilbourne, Yorkshire, England. This family is described as being a family of some note in England and in the town of Wethersfield, Connecticut. Thomas and his family embarked for New England on the ship *Increase* in April 1634, eventually migrating to Litchfield.

Timothy and Aaron Kilborn's father, Joseph, fought in the American Revolution in Connecticut along with his father and brother.

Possible ancestors of Gideon and Joseph Dudley were William Dudley and his wife Jane Lutman. They left Ockley, County Surrey, England, on May 20, 1639, on the *St. John*, the first boat to go directly to Connecticut, and settled in Guilford. Their child William was born at sea and appears in early records of Guilford as a cordwainer by trade. In 1747 members of the family moved to Cornwall, Connecticut.

From this point on, the history of the Dudley family is tied by popular legend to the small village of Dudleytown near Cornwall. According to legend, Dudleytown is home to supernatural activities, ghosts and untimely deaths. Some blame these events on the "Dudley curse," based on an early incident in England involving the beheading of a Dudley by the king. A 1989 article in the *New York Times* told the story of the founding of the town and the relationship of the Dudley family to its demise.[113] Much of this has been denounced by the Cornwall Historical Society, which has attempted to discourage ghost hunters and other thrill seekers from visiting the site.

Dudleytown was originally settled in 1738 and named Owlsbury for the many owls that lived there. In 1747 Abiel and Barzillai Dudley, French and Indian War veterans, settled there and were later joined by Martin, Gideon and Obijah Dudley. From genealogical records, it appears that Abiel and Barzillai were brothers and that their brother Israel was the father of Martin, who was the father of kidnappers Gideon and Joseph.

Martin was married in Cornwall, Connecticut, in 1763 to Anna Dudley, perhaps a cousin. His son Gideon was born in 1765. There is no Joseph Dudley listed in Connecticut vital town records as a child of Martin; it is probable that Joseph was born after Martin left Connecticut.

A story of the interactions between the Dudley and Roswell Franklin families illustrates the complicated and shifting alliances among the Connecticut settlers. On April 7, 1781, the family of Roswell Franklin Sr. was abducted by Iroquois. Gideon Dudley was one of eight pursuing the thirteen braves. Mrs. Franklin and her children—Olive, age thirteen; Susanna; Stephen, age four; and Ichabod, age eighteen months—had been abducted while Franklin was away, and when he came home, he sounded an alarm at Wilkes-Barre. During a battle two days later, Gideon was wounded in the arm. Mrs. Franklin was killed and was buried in the woods, but the rest of the family built a raft to float down the river and home.

Seven years later, on July 29, 1788, Captain Roswell Franklin Jr. led a party that ambushed and fatally wounded Joseph Dudley as he was trying to evade capture for the kidnapping of Pickering. This captain was the son of Roswell Franklin, whose family Joseph's brother Gideon had rescued in 1781. Roswell Jr. was not with the family when they were captured, having been abducted by the Iroquois in 1779. He was traded by the British in 1781 and arrived home just after his mother was killed. It is likely that he knew the Dudley family and also knew that the brother of the man he shot in 1788 had rescued his own brother and sisters in 1781. Nevertheless, he pursued and shot Joseph following the kidnapping. Joseph later died of his wounds.

Gideon was wounded again during the kidnapping. On July 4, Pickering wrote in his diary that "the High Sheriff with D Shff Ross & about 18 men had met with 3 of the boys & exch. some shot, in wh. Gid. Dudley was wounded in the hand, & had his rifle stock split in pieces."[114]

With the wounding of Gideon and the death of Joseph, the only two kidnappers to be shot, perhaps the curse of the Dudley family continued.

JOHN HYDE JR.

John Hyde was frequently described as a leader of the kidnappers. Kidnapper Benedict Satterlee stated in his deposition that John Hyde told him that if he did not join the kidnappers, he would not be able live in the settlement, so he agreed. During the kidnapping, the reward for Hyde's capture was $300, while the other kidnappers' captors were to receive $100. On the day Pickering was released, John Hyde was the primary author of an apology to Timothy Pickering from several of the kidnappers and their associates.

Hyde was undoubtably related to Ezekiel Hyde of Norwich, Connecticut, who was listed in Craft's history of Bradford County as one of the leaders of the Wild Yankees. The relationship of John to Ezekiel and to other members of the Hyde family is not readily apparent.

A Hyde family immigrated from England about 1633. The possible ancestor of the Wyoming Valley family, William, appears in records of Hartford, Connecticut, in 1636. The names of his descendants Jabez, Ezekiel and Elisha Hyde are associated with the Delaware and Susquehannah Companies in the history of Norwich. Hyde family members who were in the Valley at the time of the kidnapping include William Hyde, a husbandman from Wilkesborough; Peleg Hyde, who was asked by Timothy Pickering to sell him his land in Wilkes-Barre; Jabez Hyde, who married the daughter of John Jenkins, Lydia; and John Hyde, mentioned as an "original settler and sufferer" in a "Proceeding of the Susquehannah Company Commissioners" in 1787. There are several listings of a John Hyde Jr. suggesting they were father and son.[115]

WILKES JENKINS

Wilkes, born in 1767, was the younger brother of John and Stephen Jenkins. He did not stand out among the kidnappers but raised the same issues, signed the same documents and was generally affiliated with the other fourteen. As mentioned above, he was one of those charged with riot and unlawful assembly in the destruction of the Zebulon Marcy home, indicating more than passing interest in the more violent pursuits of the group.

As stated above, the Jenkins family were Quakers originally living in the Plymouth Colony. John Jenkins Sr.—the father of Wilkes, John and Stephen—was an early proprietor of the Susquehannah Company, among those who surveyed the Wyoming Valley in 1753 and one of the signers of the land sale agreement with the Haudenosaunee in 1754. He had been present at the first Wyoming massacre in 1763 and was one of the First Forty who came to settle the area in 1769. At that time, Wilkes would have been two years old.

As the much younger brother of the leader John Jenkins (b. 1751), Wilkes may have had a familial obligation to participate in the Yankee wars with the Pennamites.

Ira Manvil/Manvill/Manville

In February 1787, Ira Manvil was listed in the Susquehannah Company papers as a saddler from Kingston. Genealogical records indicate he was born on June 29, 1763, in Woodbury, Connecticut, making him twenty-five when Pickering was abducted.

The oral history of this family is different from that of the other kidnappers: Ira's apparent ancestor Nicholas Manville Sr., born 1712 in Picardie, France, was a tailor responsible for sail making and repair on a French boat when he jumped ship early in the eighteenth century. He acquired land in Woodbury, Connecticut, in 1735 or 1736 and appears in church records of the time. An article in the *American Genealogist* in 1958 reports that in 1735, Nicholas and his future wife, Mary Murray, were fined £2 10s. and costs for the misdemeanor of conception prior to matrimony. Their second child, Nicholas Junior, father of Ira, was born later, in 1738.

Ira's father, Nicholas Jr., moved his family from Branford, Connecticut, to Plymouth, Wyoming Valley. He enlisted in the Revolution under Random and Durkee in September 1776 and was reported to be in Valley Forge with Continental forces when he returned to the Wyoming Valley to protect his home and family. He was one of the settlers killed at the Battle of Wyoming in 1778, at age forty; his name, spelled "Nichols Manvil," is on the Wyoming Massacre Monument in Luzerne County, Pennsylvania.

SLAIN IN BATTLE

ANDERSON DANA	HENRY JOHNSON	JOSEPH SHAW
JAMES DIVINE	WILLIAM LESTER	ABRAM SHAW
GEORGE DOWNING	JOSHUA LANDON	DARIUS SPAFFORD
LEVI DUNN	DANL. LAWRENCE	LEVI SPENCER
WILLIAM DUNN	WM. LAWRENCE	JAMES SPENCER
DUTCHER	FRANCIS LEDYARD	JOSIAH SPENCER
BENJAMIN FINCH	JAMES LOCK	ELEAZER SPRAGUE
JOHN FINCH	CONRAD LOWE	AARON STARK
DANIEL FINCH	JACOB LOWE	DANIEL STARK
ELISHA FISH	NICHOLS MANVIL	JOSEPH STAPLES
CORNES. FITCHETT	JOB MARSHALL	REUBEN STAPLES
ELIPH. FOLLET	NEW MATHEWSON	RUFUS STEVENS
THOMAS FOXEN	C. MC CARTEE	JAMES STEVENSON
JOHN FRANKLIN	A. MEELEMAN	NAILER SWEED
THOMAS FULLER	ROBERT MC INTIRE	ICHABOD TUTTLE
STEPHEN FULLER	ANDREW MILLARD	JOHN VANWEE
GARDENER	JOHN MURPHY	ABRAM VANGORDER
GEORGE GORE	JOSEPH OGDEN	ELIHU WATERS
GREEN	JOHN PIERCE	BARTHOLW. WEEKS
SAML. HUTCHINSON	ABEL PALMER	JONATHAN WEEKS
WILLIAM HAMMOND	SILAS PARKE	PHILIP WEEKS
SILAS HARVEY	WILLIAM PARKER	PETER WHEELER
BENJAMIN HATCH	HENRY PENCIL	STEPHEN WHITON
CYPRIAN HEBERD	NOAH PETTEBONE, JR.	ESEN WILCOX
LEVI HICKS	JEREMIAH ROSS	JOHN WILLIAMS
JAMES HOPKINS	WILLIAM REYNOLDS	ELIHU WILLIAMS, JR.
NATHL. HOWARD	ELISHA RICHARDS	RUFUS WILLIAMS
JOHN HUTCHINS	ELIAS ROBERTS	AZIBAH WILLIAMS
ISRAEL INMAN	ENOS ROCKWAY	JOHN WARD
ELIJAH INMAN	TIMOTHY ROSE	JOHN WILSON
JOSEPH JENNINGS	JOSEPH SHAW	PARKER WILSON
SAMUEL JACKSON	CONSTANT SEARLES	NATHAN WADE
ROBERT JAMESON	ABEL SEELEY	WM. WOODRINGER
		OZIAS YALE

ESON BROCKWAY	KINGSLEY COMSTOCK	NOAH PETTEBONE SR.
JOSEPH BUDD	ZIPPORAH HIBBARD	GERSHOM PRINCE
CAMPBELL	ALEXANDER McMILLAN	GAMALIEL TRUESDALE

Ira Manvil's father is included among those memorialized by the Wyoming Monument.
Photograph by Stan Fox.

Benedict Satterlee

Benedict Satterlee's role was not a major one, and he later expressed ambivalence about the whole affair. His big brother Elisha, in charge of the family after their parents died, was a supporter of John Franklin and an active Wild Yankee in forays against the Pennamites but stated that "he would rather have given all he was worth in the world than that his brother Benedict should have been in the scrape."[116] Benedict was teaching school in Athens when Ira Manvil and Frederick Budd came to him and told him about the kidnapping.

The apparent Satterlee family progenitor Benedict Satterlee was born at St. Ide, Exeter, England, in 1655 or 1656. According to genealogical records, the family claims descent from a vicar and a knight in England, and the original estate in Suffolk still has the Satterlee escutcheon over the central arch of the church.

Benedict's forefather is described in genealogical records as a captain of a ship, either trading between England and New England or in the English navy. In either case, he allegedly fell in love with a widow in Connecticut, Rebecca Bemis Minter Dimond, resigned his command and spent the rest of his life with her.

Benedict Satterlee's father, Benedict, great-grandson of the first Satterlee in New England, was one of the original forty settlers of the Wyoming Valley. The elder Benedict Satterlee was present, but not killed, at the first massacre in 1763. He died prior to 1778 during "some of the troubles incident to the settlement," leaving a widow and six children. The widow, "fleeing with her children after the massacre, perished in the wilderness of fatigue,"[117] leaving her eldest son, Elisha, to raise the other children.

Kidnapper Benedict was born in 1763 in Plainfield, Windham County, Connecticut. He became a schoolteacher in the town of Athens and married the daughter of Captain Joseph Spaulding, Welthia.

Daniel Taylor

According to some genealogical records, Daniel Taylor was born around 1760, making him twenty-eight at the time of the kidnapping, somewhat old to be considered a "Boy." In the "Declaration in Support of the Laws of Pennsylvania," he is listed as a resident of Jacobs Plains who chose *not* to

The Flight of the Survivors of the Wyoming Massacre through "the Shades of Death." Scribner's Magazine, 1902. Collection of Stephen B. Killian, Esq.

sign the declaration. John Taylor (probably a relative) did sign as a resident of Kingston and Exeter.

During the kidnapping, Pickering wrote in his diary that Daniel Taylor had been schooling him in farming methods:

> *D. Taylor says that sows should be very moderately fed after pigging the first weeks, or will get cloyed & not eat well & their pigs will never be fat. Oxen continue to grow till 6 & 7 years old—often worked in Connecticut till 12 years old. They plow among corn with oxen, but with a long yoke & the staple not in the middle, so as better to avoid hurting the corn with the chain. No driver necessary, when oxen well broken. Price of an ox cart compleat in Con is £5. He says heifers often have their first calves at 2 years old—but then go farrow the next year.*[118]

Taylor was also one of the kidnappers who insisted that Pickering be put in chains.

A New England settler named John Taylor may be the ancestor of Daniel. He was born in 1605 in England and settled in Lynn, Massachusetts, about 1630. Oral history of the family is that he came from Haverhill, Suffolk, England, and that his wife and children died on the voyage to Massachusetts. He married a widow with two children, and in 1639 the family removed to Windsor, Connecticut. There he had two more sons, John (1641) and Thomas (1643), but he did not live to raise them. In November 1645, John made a will predicated on an anticipated voyage to England. The will was not probated until 1694, because after John left for England in the winter of 1645, he was never seen again.

John Taylor was one of about seventy settlers who had formed a company, the Ship Fellowship, which financed the building of a 150-ton ship to carry furs and other goods to England. The "great shippe" was reportedly ill-built, "walt-sided" and ill laden, with the lighter objects on the bottom. It left in a bitter winter and had to chop a path through the ice for three miles in order to get out to sea.

The ship never returned, but a ghost ship was reported to have appeared two years later. The "Phantom Ship" was memorialized by Henry Longfellow.

John Taylor Jr. was born in Windsor, Connecticut, about 1641. At about age eighteen he moved to Northampton, Massachusetts, where he was killed while pursuing a raiding party of about fifty Natives and twenty Frenchmen who had attacked a nearby village. The possible father of kidnapper Daniel Taylor, Reuben Taylor II, a direct descendant of the original John Taylor, moved back and forth between Connecticut, Massachusetts and New York. A newspaper report in 1924 stated that he was an original Connecticut settler in northeastern Pennsylvania and that he had served in the state militia for New York and Connecticut and "on the high seas as a Revolutionary soldier."[119] Rueben had ten or eleven children. Preserved Taylor of this family signed, with Daniel, the petition to Pennsylvania to recognize the land rights of Connecticut claimants in February 1787.

A history of the town of Eaton, originally part of Tunkhannock, mentions another possible ancestor for Daniel Taylor. Three descendants of another person named John Taylor, born in 1639 in Chedison, Suffolk, England came to the area from Connecticut about the same time as Zebulon Marcy. These Taylors, about the same age as Daniel, were Obadiah (b. 1763), Aaron (b. 1762) and John (b. 1759) Taylor. They could have been relatives of Daniel.

John Whitcomb

John Whitcomb played a minor role in the kidnapping. John's brother Joel, according to his later testimony, had been asked by John Hyde to sign a "paper of association" with the kidnappers, but he declined.

John was only thirteen years old when he enlisted in the Continental army in Connecticut with his father and two of his brothers. He stayed in the service for five years, serving under Colonel Zebulon Butler in 1782. His family was in Connecticut during the Wyoming Massacre.

John's apparent ancestor John Whitcomb of Taunton, Somerset, came to New England in 1635; his daughter Joanne, age three, died off Nova Scotia as the *Hopewell* arrived. The family lived in Connecticut until John's father, Job, moved to Hemlock Bottom (now Scottsville) in the Wyoming Valley about 1787 with his sons John, Hiram, Joel and Solomon.

David Woodward

From Pickering's journals, it appears that David was friendly toward the captive. Pickering mentions David Woodward in his journal: "Woodward brought me a letter dated the 8th from Mr. Bowman, informing of the health of the family & that the articles I requested are sent to March's [Marcy's]."[120] David instructed Pickering in the arts of farming and fence building, telling

Pickering he knew all about farming from his childhood in Vermont and Massachusetts, and Pickering wrote it all down.

Historical records link David to the Woodward family who came to New England on the boat *James* in 1635 with the Reverend Richard Mather, grandfather of the well-known, celebrated Puritan theologian Cotton Mather. Henry Woodward, born in 1607 in Lancashire, England, married the reverend's daughter Elizabeth and remained in Dorchester, Massachusetts, until 1660, when he moved to Northampton. In Northampton he became one of the "seven pillars" of the church.

David's father, Captain David Woodward, married Temperance Kilborn and moved his family to Randolph, Orange County, Vermont. David was born in 1764.

On August 20, David Woodward and John Whitcomb wrote a letter to Pickering asking him to pardon them. On September 5, Pickering responded:

> *'Tis in vain for any of the party, excepting such as have become States Evidences, to expect pardons, before they have surrendered themselves to justice nor even then.... Government are exasperated by the repeated violences committed by a few turbulent men in this county, and...is determined to punish in an exemplary manner the persons who shall be convicted of the late audacious & flagrant violation of the laws of the rights of peaceable citizens.... The offenders are to be prosecuted for a* riot *only; whereas the crime of which you & the rest of the party have been guilty is clearly* high treason. *Of this I am satisfied by the examination I have made of the law since my return.... Government therefore have manifested great lenity & mercy towards the offenders in directing that they be prosecuted only for a riot, when they might be charged with high treason, &, on conviction, be punished with death.*[121]

Pickering also stated in his letter that if David and John wished to "live again in Pennsylvania" they should surrender.

Chapter 11

THE FATE OF THE KIDNAPPERS
AND OF COLONEL PICKERING

W ithin days of the kidnapping, in the dead of night, there was a knock on the door of Benjamin Earl's cabin. His new wife, a buxom lass who was twice his size, stuck her panicked spouse in the feather bed, where he sank to the bottom, and placed her considerable self on top of him so that it appeared only one person was in the bed. She then said to Constable Westover:

> *"Come in, who is there?"*
> *"Westover! Come, Earl, you are my prisoner," and entered the room with a light.*
> *"For shame, Mr. Westover," said Mrs. Earl, "I [am] here a lone woman to be so encroached upon."*
> *"But where is Ben?"*
> *"You know he was expecting the writ and needn't think he was such a fool as to be at home—he has more wit than that, I hope."*
> *Satisfied the lady was alone, Westover retired.*[122]

Benjamin's part in the kidnapping of Timothy Pickering had come home to roost.

There had been calls for the capture of the kidnappers since the abduction of Pickering.

PENNSYLVANIA

By the *Vice President* and the *Supreme Executive Council* of the Commonwealth of Pennfylvania

A PROCLAMATION.

WHEREAS by depofitions taken according to law, It appears that feveral evil difpofed persons have confpired to obftruct the execution of the laws in the county of Luzerne, and have violently feized and carried off the perfon of Timothy Pickering, efquire, an officer of government, whom they ftill retain as prifoner; AND WHEREAS it is of great importance to the good people of this Commonwealth, that fuch heinous offenders fhould be brought to condign punifhment – WE have thought fit to offer, and do hereby offer, a Public Reward of *Three Hundred Dollars* for apprehending and fecuring John Jenkins, *Three Hundred Dollars* for apprehending and fecuring John Hyde, and the fum of *One Hundred Dollars* for apprehending and fecuring each and every of the following named perfons, viz. *Daniel Earl, Benjamin Earl*, _____ *Cady, Wilkes Jenkins, Jofeph Dudley, Gideon Dudley, David Woodward, John Whitcomb, Timothy Kilburne,* and *Thomas Kinney*, or for apprehending and fecuring any other perfons who fhall be convicted of aiding and affifting in taking of the faid Timothy Pickering – The reward for apprehending and fecuring any of the above named perfons, will be paid on their being delivered to the jail of the county of Northampton: and all Judges, Juftices, Sheriffs, and Conftables, are hereby ftrictly enjoined and required to make diligent fearch and enquiry after, and to ufe their utmoft endeavours to apprehend and fecure the faid offenders, fo that they may be dealt with according to law.

    Given in Council, under the Hand of the Honorable PETER MUHLENBERG, Efquire, Vice Prefident, and the Seal of the State, at Philadelphia, this eighth day of July, in the Year of Our Lord one Thousand, feven Hundred and Eighty eight.

PETER MUHLENBERG.

Atteft   CHARLES RIDDLE Sec'ty

Proclamation in the *Pennsylvania Packet*, Philadelphia, PA, August 2, 1788. *Reproduction by Kathleen A. Earle.*

Pickering's abduction was one of the last major hostile actions taken in the Yankee-Pennamite dispute. After Pickering was released, Pennsylvania authorities described the kidnapping quite differently than did the kidnappers or even Pickering himself. During his captivity, in a letter to his wife, Pickering wrote, "I live as they do: they are civil and take pains to make me as comfortable as my situation will admit."[123] His diary generally provides a picture of begrudging respect of Pickering by his captors, rather than the abuse later alleged.

At the end of his captivity, Pickering had agreed to forgive the kidnappers if they promised to obey the laws of Pennsylvania. But when the young men tried to get Pickering to intercede for them with the authorities, he declined, unless they would give him the names of their leaders, which they refused to do. He continued to refer to them as "ruffians" in his voluminous correspondence on the subject and eventually called for their full punishment under the law.

The Boys realized their error, and on July 15, the same day they released him, John Hyde and eight of the other kidnappers, along with Nathan and Benjamin Abbot, who had joined the kidnappers after Pickering was taken, wrote a letter to Pickering requesting leniency:

> *As you have generously declared your willingness to forgive us for the great injury we have done you, in seizing and keeping you a prisoner in the manner we have done, from the 26th of June last to this day on the single condition that in future we pay a due obedience to the laws & government of the state of Pennsylvania in which we live: We hereby express our thankfulness for your kindness in this matter, & solemnly engage that we will never hereafter disturb the peace of said state, nor of the county of Luzerne which is a part thereof, but, while we dwell therein, will in all respects conduct ourselves as peaceable and faithful citizens.*[124]

The petition was signed by "Ira Manvill, Benedick Satterlee, Timothy Kilbourn, Benjamin Earll, Daniel Earll, Solomon Earl, John S. Whitcomb, Nathan Abet, Benjamin Abet,[125] David Woodard, John Hyde Jn" and "John Tuttle," whose name was crossed out. Tuttle had embedded himself as a spy in the kidnapping group and later took part in a posse to capture the kidnappers. On July 29 Pickering wrote to Benjamin Franklin, "Tuttle, in particular, has very great merit, for his zeal and perseverance....Having made the party believe that he had joined them in heart, as well as person, it was necessary for him to sign [the petition] with them."[126]

A similar petition on the same date, to the Pennsylvania Council, stated that the petitioners were now "sensable of their error" and asked for the Council to "pass by" their offense:

> *They repeat With sorrow that it is a great offence against the state by violent seasing and unlawfully keeping prison[er] an innosent man, and an officer commissioned by governme[nt] nevertheless, your petitioners humbly hope they may be forgiv[en] on the deep and hartfelt repentance which they now profes[s] Assuring and assuring your honours that they have ben misi[nformed] and misled by men in whose Judgment and advise they have ben want to place an entire confidence; on this further assuran[ce] also of their future fidelity to the state, and of their readi[ness] to enter into such engagement for that end as your honours shall require.*[127]

It was signed by the aforementioned signatories plus these additional men: "Daniel Taylor, Gideon Dudley, Joseph Dudley, Friadreek Budd, Wils Jenkins, Aaron Kilborn, Wm Carney, Zebulon Cady" and "Noah Phelps." As with the other petition, the name of "John Tuttle" was on the document but had been crossed out.

Nevertheless, prosecution of the kidnappers and their allies continued and was legislated by the Pennsylvania delegates to the Continental Congress on July 22. By this time, the Boys had begun to scatter. Search parties were formed, and they were hunted down.

Ira Manvil and Benedict Satterlee were arrested following their capture on July 18. They were jailed in Easton.[128] Members of the posse were later awarded seventy-five pounds, to be distributed among the captors, for their apprehension.

Joseph Dudley was involved in the July 29 skirmish with Captain Roswell Franklin and his men described above. Franklin, John Tuttle and others were lying in wait when Joseph Dudley and Nathan and Benjamin Abbot appeared. According to Tuttle, they hailed the boys, but when they did not surrender, Joseph Dudley was shot and ran about four hundred yards, shouting, "Run boys, run like thunder," before he fell down. Tuttle and the others put him in a canoe and took him down the river to Wilkes-Barre. He was brought before Pickering, who wrote in a letter to Benjamin Franklin on July 29 that Joseph was "dangerously" wounded.[129]

On July 30 John Hyde and Frederick Budd were on their way to Tioga when twenty soldiers were sent to apprehend them, but they "stole a canoe and made their escape a little before evening."[130] Hyde was finally captured about forty miles above Tioga but asked to send for his clothes; the boy who went for the clothes alerted his comrades, and they rescued him. During the rescue, a horse of one of the pursuers was killed.

In August, Pickering reported that most of the Boys had fled through the Great Swamp, toward Tioga, to the New York Finger Lakes or to Connecticut. Four had been jailed. Besides Ira Manvill and Benedict Saterlee in the Easton jail, Benjamin Earl and Joseph Dudley were in the Wilkes-Barre jail, where Dudley died of his wounds.

Benjamin turned state's evidence and testified on July 19. In his deposition he attempted to clarify the innocence of those involved directly in the kidnapping, insisting that others, such as Stephen Jenkins and John Jenkins, came up with the plan and that it was done only in order to secure the release of John Franklin from jail. He described Pickering's abduction and stay in the woods, and then added that the Boys had received a letter indicating that Colonel McKinstry said he would provide for Colonel Pickering if they could not hold him; that McKinstry had provisions of corn available to them; and that if the Boys lost some of their lands, McKinstry would give them back. Benjamin also said that some of the Boys had been told Colonel John Livingston encouraged keeping Pickering prisoner.[131]

The September 2 indictment from the Pennsylvania authorities presented the kidnappers in the most severe terms, describing a riotous band "having their faces painted and disfigured" who forcefully "an assault did make, and the said Timothy Pickering then and there did beat, wound, and evilly treat," putting him "cruelly and ignominiously" in chains while exposing him to insults and bad weather.[132]

The fate of the leaders of the kidnappers was described in Pickering's own hand in November of 1788. John Franklin, John Jenkins, Zerah Beach and John McKinstry, instigators of the kidnapping, were indicted for high treason; Joseph Kilborn and Stephen Jenkins, who abetted the kidnappers, were sentenced to pay a fine of one hundred dollars and costs and be imprisoned for six months. Pickering was especially pleased with the prosecution of Jenkins, whom he held responsible for the house arrest of Pickering's wife right after Franklin was jailed.

The sentence to the latter gave particular satisfaction at my house; he was the unfeeling rascal who ordered my wife to prepare herself & children to move in one hour for Tioga. The Chief Justice animadverted on their conduct, told them that they had been guilty of High treason, and that in any country in Europe they would all be hanged, and it was to the mildness of the government of Pennsylvania they were indebted for the light punishment now ordered."[133]

John Franklin was released on bail in March 1789 and was never brought to trial. While the indictment for treason was still hanging over him in 1792, he was elected high sheriff of Luzerne County. He went on to serve as a member of the assembly from Luzerne County for several years and moved to his farm in Athens, where he died in 1831, never having accepted or recognized Pennsylvania title to his land. His heirs were required to purchase the land after his death. Today, the gravestone of Franklin and his wife, Abigail, on the site of his home in Athens, stands beside a large memorial stone dedicated to Franklin.

The kidnappers were tried and all found guilty of riot. Most were, "on account of their poverty & because misled by old men, mildly dealt with." They were fined seven to nine pounds plus costs, and those who were captured were put in jail. Timothy Kilborn and Zebulon Cady were sentenced to one to three months' imprisonment.[134] Relatives who had assisted in the abduction were jailed, while some, including Joseph Earl, were discharged the same day for lack of evidence. Pickering wrote that Martin Dudley (father of Gideon and Joseph Dudley) and Joseph Kilborn (father of Timothy and Aaron Kilborn) had families in distress and were "miserably poor" and suggested they be allowed to post bail.[135]

In 1796 and 1799, respectively, Ira Manvil and Benedict Satterlee, who had been jailed, were given land by the Susquehannah Company, for "services rendered." Manvil was given one thousand acres and Satterlee one half-share, or three hundred acres, of land. A smaller piece, two hundred acres, was given to John Hyde Jr. in 1794.

Ira Manvil stayed in Plymouth, Luzerne, where his name appears on census and tax records in 1800. Satterlee apparently moved to Morris, New York, where he died on January 8, 1813.

Original gravestone for John Franklin and his wife, Abigail, and memorial for John Franklin in Athens, Pennsylvania. *Photograph by Kathleen A. Earle.*

In 1791 there was a "Daniel Taylor" who was an overseer of roads in Providence, Luzerne. This might be Daniel Taylor the kidnapper, although Pickering reported Taylor "fled thro' the Great-Swamp" with Daniel and Solomon Earl and Zebulon Cady. It is unclear where John Hyde was located after 1794.

Benjamin Earl, who had turned state's witness, remained in Tunkhannock, where he continued to insist on the legal right to his land. A petition to Congress from Connecticut claimants in 1802 asking for redress was signed by Benjamin Earll, along with Zebulon Butler, John Franklin, Stephen Jenkins and several others.

By 1800, many Yankees who remained in the valley were attempting to reach an agreement with the Pennsylvania authorities, even relinquishing their Connecticut deeds and purchasing deeds from the "Pennsylvania Landholders," which handled state titles to the land. This was not a smooth transition, however, as many of the Yankees still refused to submit to Pennsylvania law and harassed, beat or even shot at Pennsylvania agents and surveyors. Eventually the landholder's association ended much of the opposition by asking settlers to pay what the land was worth "in a state of nature" rather than as developed land. The struggle over property, reports Moyer, became a battle about price.[136]

While Solomon and Daniel fled to New York, Joseph Earl initially stayed in Tunkhannock and appears, along with Benjamin, in the 1790 Luzerne census. A Daniel Earl also appears in that census, but it is unclear if this was the elder Daniel Earl, the kidnapper Daniel Earl or even a different Daniel Earl.

PICKERING AND THE HAUDENOSAUNEE

By the end of the kidnapping trials, Timothy Pickering was close to financial ruin. With six young sons to support, he tried to find a political appointment to support himself and his family. After several failed attempts, in 1790 he was appointed a special emissary to a group of Seneca living along the Susquehanna River. This was the beginning of a five-year career as an Indian diplomat. One author stated, "Red Jacket, no mean intellect himself, sizing up Pickering for what he was," gave him the name Kanehsadeh, which means "on the side of a hill."[137] As Washington's emissary, Pickering found that his first major task was to quell the continuing anger of Seneca leaders due to the loss of their lands based on the Fort Stanwix Treaty.

On October 22, 1784, the Treaty of Fort Stanwix had been signed near Oneida Lake, New York. It imposed peace on the four hostile tribes of the Haudenosaunee—Mohawk, Onondaga, Cayuga and Seneca—and assured the Oneida and Tuscarora of continued peaceful possession of their land. The treaty also allowed for the United States and private companies to take or purchase Haudenosaunee lands, especially those of the Seneca. Much of that land was purchased by Oliver Phelps in 1788 as the Phelps and Gorham Purchase. Famous Seneca chiefs Farmer's Brother, Cornplanter and Red Jacket met with Pickering in 1790 and claimed that Phelps had defrauded the Seneca, and they demanded the return of their land. Pickering was convinced that something had gone wrong in this purchase and agreed that the Seneca may have been defrauded, perhaps with the assistance of the Mohawk leader Joseph Brant. Moreover, he felt that Native people were easily defrauded because they were unable to resist the temptation of alcohol. He believed he could defend the Seneca against their own naivete by creating the position of superintendent of the Six Nations, with the responsibility of acting in the interest of the Haudenosaunee. He wanted to make sure the indigenous people survived but believed this would only happen if they adopted mainstream European ways: becoming farmers, learning to read English, and so on. Pickering's misguided policies hastened the evolution of the Haudenosaunee into talented connoisseurs of living in two worlds.

Pickering's paternalism toward the Haudenosaunee and other Native people over the next few years was well regarded by the leaders of the young United States, and he was welcomed back into the halls of power and prestige. In 1794, he was appointed Washington's secretary of war.

Chapter 12

ESCAPE TO THE LAKES

S ome of the Yankees who fled prosecution for the kidnapping left the Wyoming Valley for good. Several relocated to the Finger Lakes of New York, recently vacated by the Haudenosaunee with the help of Sullivan's campaign. These included kidnappers Solomon and Daniel Earl, Frederick Budd, Gideon Dudley, Timothy Kilborn, Wilkes Jenkins and possibly David Woodward. They were joined by family members implicated in the kidnapping. John Whitcomb initially went to the Finger Lakes but later returned to Wyoming. Zebulon Cady, who, according to Pickering, reportedly "Fled thro' the Great Swamp" with Daniel and Solomon Earl, may have gone to Connecticut.

Kidnapper John Whitcomb married Sarah Marsh in Geneva, New York, on December 15, 1789, the first recorded marriage of non-Natives in the town. In 1790, he was living next to Timothy and Aaron's father, Joseph Kilborn, in Canandaigua, New York. John and Sarah had several children in Geneva and around 1810 he moved back to Hemlock Bottom (now Scottville), Pennsylvania, where his father had first moved from Connecticut. John Whitcomb died and was buried in Hemlock Bottom in 1832.

Besides John Whitcomb and Joseph Kilborn, early records of Canandaigua include the names of Gideon Dudley and his father, Martin, and Timothy Kilborn. When he died in 1817, Joseph Kilborn was living in Delaware, Ontario, Canada. Timothy and his younger brother Aaron were both living in London, Ontario, at the time of their deaths, in 1864 and 1833, respectively.

A Daniel Earl appears in an early journal kept by settler Alexander Coventry, who describes Earl as a squatter in the area between Cayuga and Seneca Lakes in 1791. From historical records, this looks like it was the Haudenosaunee village of Kanadia, now within the area of Romulus. Living in his neighborhood near Seneca Lake, Coventry wrote, was Daniel Earl, who had built a log cabin, made some improvements and sowed the first crop of wheat in the area, on military lot number 11; a Mr. Budd, "a son-in-law of Mr. Earl," was living nearby, wrote Coventry, as well as a Mr. Tubbs.[138]

"Mr. Budd" was probably Frederick Budd, whose name is on land and census records in the Finger Lakes region, living near Daniel and Solomon Earl. It is unclear from genealogical records if he was a son-in-law of Daniel Earl.

"Mr. Tubbs" was probably the actual son-in-law of Daniel Earl of Pomfret and Tunkhannock. Daniel had a daughter, Molly, who married Yankee Enos Tubbs and is buried next to her father, Daniel Earl, near Seneca Lake. The graves of Daniel Earl, his wife, Dorcas, and of Molly Tubbs today rest side by side on a windy hill in the town of Benton. Daniel Earl was also described in historical records as an early farmer in the town of Geneva, New York, "with his son, Solomon." This suggests that Solomon was the son of the elder Daniel Earl rather than the son of Joseph Earl, since conventions of the day sometimes made "son" and "nephew" synonymous.

A younger Daniel Earl also appears in records of the area, purchasing land in Ulysses, New York, near Cayuga Lake, in 1801 and living in Ulysses in the federal census of 1810. This may be the kidnapper Daniel Earl.

After the kidnapping, Pickering reported that Wilkes Jenkins had "Fled to the Lakes" with Frederick Budd. In 1790, Jenkins was living in Chemung, New York, and in 1800 in Tioga. For the next thirty years census records show him in Elmira Village, Tioga, New York. At one point he had five hundred acres of land, where he raised three children: Zina, Archibald and Nancy. Wilkes died in 1838.

There was a "Woodward" listed, along with Gideon Dudley and Solomon Earl, in an early list of settlers in the Geneva-Canandaigua area, but it is not evident if this is David Woodward. However, David was married to Betsy Tubbs, possibly a relative of Enos, who was married to Molly Earl and immigrated to New York with the Earls.

Before 1800, Tunkhannock still contained many rough-hewn cabins, but compared to upstate New York, the Wyoming Valley was a place of relative ease and sophistication. The town of Wilkes-Barre, home of Pickering, had many substantial houses and businesses in 1789. When they got to New York, the Connecticut Yankees found that conditions were harsh. Geneva was described as:

> *A small, unhealthy village, containing about fifteen houses, all log except three, and about twenty families. It is built partly on the acclivity of a hill, partly on a flat, with deep marshes north of the town, to the presence of which ill health is attributed. The accommodations by Patterson on the lake margin were decent, but repose was troubled by the presence of gamblers and vermin.*[139]

The relationship of early settlers in the Finger Lakes to the local Haudenosaunee is illuminated in a narrative about Solomon Earl's unfortunate injury. In the early spring of 1789, Solomon Earl was snoring in a cabin along the Ganargwa Creek on the Phelps and Gorham Purchase, when five Tuscarora braves and their female companion stuck their hunting rifles through holes in the cabin wall and opened fire. Earl had his hand on his breast, and a musket ball smashed through his hand and mutilated his jaw. Another sleeping man, "Mr. Baker," was killed.

John Jenkins and John Swift had purchased lot number 12, now in Palmyra, in 1788 or 1789 and were surveying it into farm lots. Their companions were Earl, Jenkins' nephew (through his wife, Bethia) Alpheus Harris and Daniel Ransom.

Swift, originally from Litchfield County, Connecticut, was a well-respected member of the Connecticut Yankee community, a revolutionary soldier in the Battle of Wyoming in 1778 and a soldier in Sullivan's campaign. He was one of the eight Yankees who pursued the Iroquois after Mrs. Roswell Franklin and her children were abducted in 1781. In 1814, he would become brigadier general of New York volunteers in the Niagara campaign and die in that war. Swift's Landing in Palmyra is named after him. He had been implicated in some of the Wild Yankees' destructive undertakings, including surrounding Pickering's house and threatening Mrs. Pickering two days after Franklin was jailed. Pickering later wrote a letter to Swift condemning the "house arrest of Mrs. Pickering," who, Pickering stated, was "of tender frame, and has an infant at her breast, but about three weeks old, besides four other children to look after." Mrs. Pickering was soon freed, but, wrote Pickering to Swift, "Let me ask What can you & those who joined you, propose to yourselves in taking up arms? Is it possible you should think Franklin's party able to withstand the power of Pennsylvania?"[140]

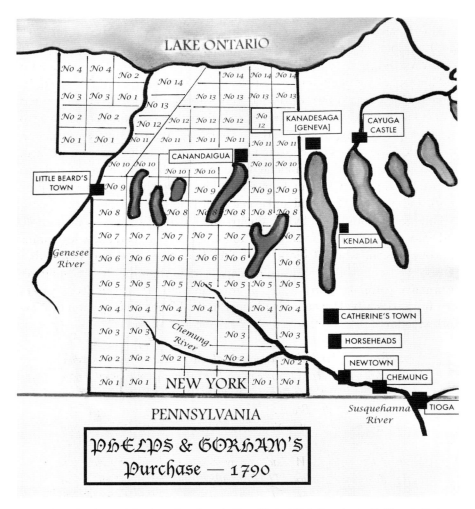

Map of the Phelps and Gorham Purchase in New York, 1790. *Drawing by Kathleen A. Earle.*

"Mr. Baker" may have been Jeremiah Baker, or a relative of Baker, who was one of the Yankees who signed a petition against what were viewed as unfair actions of Pennsylvania against the Yankees. Jenkins' nephew Alpheus Harris may have been related to Elijah Harris, who signed the same document, along with John Swift, John Jenkins, Solomon Earl, the rest of the Earls and many of the kidnappers. Daniel Ransom was probably related to Asa Ransom, an early settler of the Geneva area.

Now Ransom seized an axe, Jenkins a "Jonas staff," and they beat back the Tuscarora, capturing their rifles and a tomahawk. In the morning the Tuscarora returned while the others were taking Solomon Earl to Geneva and took all of the provisions out of the cabin, motivated, it was believed, by hunger. The Tuscarora were pursued to Newtown, where they were captured at the Chemung River. It was decided that the nearest jail was too far away to risk the captives being freed, so a lynch court was organized and an execution prescribed. The braves were taken into the woods, and one was tomahawked. The second, being "a stout athletic man," parried the blow, escaped and was followed by a posse, who caught and beat him to death with stones and pine knots. This was the "first trial and execution in the Genesee Country."[141]

The area encompassed by the Phelps and Gorham Purchase was remote and wild. Geneva, the closest village to lot number 12, had a few log cabins and one tavern, where Colonel Seth Reed provided bed and board that consisted of a loaf of bread. A ruined apple orchard, reminder of Sullivan's destructive campaign, and fields of grass and clover surrounded a picket fort. It was described by an early pioneer in the Finger Lakes region of New York as follows:

> *Soon after my father had come on west of the river, and opened a public house, other settlers began to come in.…The Indians were frequent visitors at my fathers. I used to see them often, the chiefs, Hot Bread, Jack Berry, Red Jacket, and Little Beard.…We brought in a few sheep with us…they became the especial object of the wolves. Coming out of the Wilson swamp nights, their howling would be terrific.…I could tell many stories of wild beasts in this region.…We had no way to keep fowls, but to secure them well in their roosting places. The first settlers found it very difficult to keep hogs; the bears would come out of the woods and take them by daylight.*[142]

In 1790, Solomon Earl was a ferry man at Kashong across the outlet of Seneca Lake, near Benton, for settlers on their way to Geneva. A settler by the name of Mrs. Warren describes seeing him there:

> *The next night we got to the foot of Seneca Lake—found there a man by the name of Earl; he had a log cabin, but no floor in it; we stayed there all night; Earl had a scow to ferry us across the outlet of the lake. Next morning we went home with Mrs. Reed and family—found Col. Reed at home, waiting for the arrival of his family. His house stood on the bank of the lake, in Geneva; the place then contained ten or twelve families.*[143]

Solomon Earl fought at the Niagara Frontier in the War of 1812, and it appears from genealogical records that he died in 1816 from his war injuries.

One of the Tuscarora braves, known as Turkey, carried a scar from Jenkins's staff for the rest of his life. Well known to the colonial settlers of the region, Turkey contracted smallpox during the War of 1812 and was taken by relatives to a hut in the pine woods to die.

The Tuscarora braves were part of a dwindling population in that area. In 1789, there were only a few Tuscarora living close to the surveyors, while another five hundred lived in a village, Junestrayo, on the Genesee River.

> *Surrounded by increasing numbers of White settlements, it was necessary [for the Tuscarora] to discuss policy on questions of accommodating to White culture....It was hoped that a greater respect for Indian ways and more careful honoring of treaties would be forthcoming from the White side. In a sense, this position looked toward mutual accommodation and cooperation without sacrificing independence, in the spirit of the "two-way wampum."*[144]

A description of Tuscarora braves was written in 1795 by Lady Simcoe, wife of Governor John Graves Simcoe of Ontario. Simcoe was given a governorship in Canada by the British for his service against the Continental army in the Revolution. Lady Simcoe's portrayal describes a people defeated but not destroyed, in transition from Haudenosaunee to European garb, who were beginning to assimilate aspects of the European culture that they found decorative or useful:

> *They are decked out with uncommon care, covered with rags of every description, and adorned with horse-hair, and feathers of all possible species of birds. In their ears and noses they wore rings of the most varied forms and colors. Some were dressed in European clothes, others wore laced hats, and some were naked, excepting a double apron, and painted from head to foot. In general they prefer the harshest colors, paint one leg white, and the other black or green, the body brown or yellow, the face full of red or black spots, and their eyes of different colors.*[145]

Ever the adapters and the accepters of their fate, the Haudenosaunee had begun to adopt some of the clothing and instruments of the European invaders. Today they continue to adapt and thrive in the United States and Canada. Many of their traditions have been kept alive, as they successfully live in two worlds.

Billboard at Akwesasne, New York, home of the Mohawk Nation, showing three young lacrosse players. *Photograph by Kathleen A. Earle.*

The families of the kidnappers who moved to the Finger Lakes area of New York eventually attained the status of landowners and productive citizens of the United States of America. Their descendants became lawyers, businessmen, teachers and farmers, primarily in New York. Apparently, most have successfully obscured their past association with the kidnappers of Timothy Pickering.

NOTES

Chapter 1

1. Charles Miner, *History of Wyoming in a Series of Letters from Charles Miner to His Son William Penn Miner, Esq.* (Philadelphia: J. Crissy, 1845), 421.
2. Robert J. Taylor, ed., *The Susquehannah Company Papers*, vol. 9, *1787–1788* (Ithaca, NY: Cornell University Press, 1970), 100. (Hereafter cited as *SCP 9*.)
3. Miner, *History*, 421.
4. Paul B. Moyer, *Wild Yankees: The Struggle for Independence along Pennsylvania's Revolutionary Frontier* (Ithaca, NY: Cornell University Press, 2007), 85; Taylor, *SCP 9*, 498. This was Aaron Kilborn, younger brother of kidnapper Timothy and son of Joseph Kilborn.
5. Miner, *History*, 422.
6. Miner, *History*, 423.
7. Miner, *History*, 424.
8. Miner, *History*, 424–25.
9. Taylor, *SCP 9*, 407–8.
10. Miner, *History*, 423.
11. Miner, *History*, 425.
12. Taylor, *SCP 9*, 415.

Chapter 2

13. Walter W. Woodward, "From the State Historian: The Map That Wasn't a Map," ConnecticutHistory.org, January 25, 2013, https://connecticuthistory.org/from-the-state-historian-the-map-that-wasnt-a-map/.
14. George E. McCracken, "The Connecticut Pennsylvanians," *American Genealogist* 55, no. 2 (April 1979): 73.
15. W.W. Munsell, *History of Luzerne, Lackawanna and Wyoming Counties, PA with Illustrations and Biographical Sketches of Some of Their Prominent Men and Pioneers* (New York: W.W. Munsell, 1880), 33; McCracken, *Connecticut Pennsylvanians*, 75. At this meeting, Pennsylvania paid for a piece of land between the Blue Mountain and the forks of the Susquehanna.
16. Munsell, *History*, 37; James R. Williamson and Linda A. Fossler, *The Susquehanna Frontier: Northeastern Pennsylvania during the Revolutionary Years* (Wilkes-Barre, PA: Wilkes University Press, 1997), 9; Miner, *History*, 53.

Chapter 3

17. H.C. Bradsby, ed., *History of Luzerne County, Pennsylvania with Biographical Selections* (Chicago: S.B. Nelson, 1893), 40. John and Emanuel Hoover were taken to Geneva, where the captives tried to escape; one of the brothers was killed, while the other got away.
18. Bradsby, *History of Luzerne*, 40.
19. Munsell, *History*, 36.
20. Munsell, *History*, 36.

Chapter 4

21. Munsell, *History*, 41.
22. Mrs. William (Hatsy) Eberhardt, *Hearts Nerved to Endure: The Story of Zebulon Marcy, First Settler of Tunkhannock, PA* (Tunkhannock, PA: Bicentennial Committee, Tunkhannock Junior Women's Club, 1976), 41.
23. David Craft, *History of Bradford County, Pennsylvania with Illustrations and Biographical Sketches of Some of Its Prominent Men and Pioneers* (Philadelphia: L.H. Everts, 1878), 102.

24. Craft, *History of Bradford*, 103.

25. Craft, *History of Bradford*, 104.

26. Taylor, *SCP 9*, 182. The "half-share men" owned half of a share of land, equal to three hundred acres, through the Susquehannah Company.

27. Taylor, *SCP 9*, 488.

28. Munsell, *History*, 306 B.

29. Taylor, *SCP 9*, 459. Included among the other militia officers Pickering was referring to were John Swift, major; Matin Dudley, captain; Joseph Kilborn, lieutenant; and David Woodward, ensign.

30. Bradsby, *History of Luzerne*, 153. This account also appears in H.C. Bradsby, *History of Bradford County, Pennsylvania, with Biographical Selections* (Chicago: S.B. Nelson, 1891), 133–34.

31. Oliver Smith Kinner, "An Interesting Narrative of Early Settlements by Indians and Whites in These Parts," *Lest We Forget* 12, no. 1 (September 15, 1992): 32.

32. Robert J. Taylor, ed., *The Susquehannah Company Papers*, vol. 8, *1785–1786* (Ithaca, NY: Cornell University Press, 1970), 363.

33. Gerard H. Clarfield, *Timothy Pickering and the American Republic* (Pittsburg: University of Pittsburg Press, 1980), vii.

34. Clarfield, *Timothy Pickering*, 5.

35. Clarfield, *Timothy Pickering*, 11.

36. Clarfield, *Timothy Pickering*, 66.

37. Luzerne County was named after Chevalier de la Luzerne, a French diplomat and soldier. Luzerne County was later divided into the counties of Bradford, Lackawanna, Susquehanna and Wyoming.

Chapter 5

38. Jack Brubaker, *Massacre of the Conestogas* (Charleston, SC: The History Press, 2013), 20.

39. William Henry Egle, *Some Pennsylvania Women During the War of the Revolution* (1898; repr., Baltimore, MD: Clearfield, 1993), 182–83.

40. Moyer, *Wild Yankees*, 34.

41. Bradsby, *History of Luzerne*, 37.

Chapter 6

42. Rupert Ross, *Dancing with a Ghost* (Toronto: Penguin Canada, 2006), ix.

43. Lewis Henry Morgan, *League of the Iroquois* (New York, NY: Corinth Books, 1962), 27.

44. William N. Fenton, *The Great Law and the Longhouse* (Norman: University of Oklahoma Press, 1998), 629.

45. Enrollment confers legitimate standing in each of the Haudenosaunee Six Nations and varies by Nation. All six Nations require matrilineal descent, but blood quantum varies. The Cayuga have the strictest requirements: enrollment is based on one-half Cayuga blood. In other words, you can only enroll in the Cayuga Nation if your mother is a full-blooded Cayuga.

46. A powwow is a social event and dance contest that provides tribal members opportunities to showcase their traditional dances and drumming. Powwows are usually intertribal and are held annually across the United States and Canada.

47. Peter Nabokov, ed., *Native American Testimony: A Chronicle of Indian-White Relations from Prophecy to the Present, 1492–1992* (New York: Penguin, 1991), 31.

48. Diamond Jenness, *The Indians of Canada*, 7th ed. (Toronto: University of Toronto Press, 1977), 139; Morgan, *League of the Iroquois*, 64–65, divides the fifty sachems among the Confederacy as follows: Mohawk 9, Oneida 9, Onondaga 14, Cayuga 10, Seneca 8. Two of the original Haudenosaunee sachem positions, Da-gä-no-wé-da ("Endless"), the name of the founder of the League of the Iroquois, and Hä-yo-went'-hä ("man who combs"), the speaker for Da-gä-no-wé-da, are left vacant. These are Mohawk sachems (Morgan, *League of the Iroquois*, 64–65, 101n).

49. William C. Canby Jr., *American Indian Law in a Nutshell*, 3rd ed. (St. Paul, MN: West Group, 1998), 23–25. The IRA, also known as the Wheeler-Howard Act, was designed to both protect the land of Native people and to permit the tribes to set up legal structures to help them in self-government. To assist in the latter, tribes were authorized to adopt constitutions and bylaws, which had to be approved by the United States secretary of the interior. The constitutions were expected to follow the American model of divided executive, legislative and judicial branches. For many tribes, including the Haudenosaunee, this was a major departure from their traditions. Only three of the six members of the Iroquois Confederacy (Mohawk, Oneida and Seneca) adopted the U.S. model, and even among these three, the traditional Iroquois model has survived and operates

alongside that required by the U.S. government. The Onondaga, Cayuga and Tuscarora have maintained their traditional government and have consequently suffered a lack of service and benefits from the United States.

50. Fenton, *The Great Law*, 249.

51. Harriet Maxwell Converse, *Myths and Legends of the New York State Iroquois* (Albany: University of the State of New York, State Education Department, 1908), 140–42. Converse was adopted by the Seneca and given the name Ya-ie-wa-noh ("She Who Watches Over Us").

52. Tehanetorens (Ray Fadden), *Wampum Belts of the Iroquois* (Summertown, Tennessee, 1999), 72–75. For a thorough discussion of the relevance of the two-row wampum belt over time, see Jon Larmenter, "The Meaning of *Kaswentha* and the Two Row Wampum Belt in Haudenosaunee (Iroquois) History: Can Indigenous Oral Tradition Be Reconciled with the Documentary Record?" *Journal of Early American History* 3 (2013), 82–109, http://honorthetworow.org/wp-content/uploads/2012/01/The-Meaning-of-Kaswentha-and-the-Two-Row.pdf.

53. For more information on the Renewal Campaign, see https://honorthetworow.org.

54. James E. Seaver, *The Life of Mary Jemison*, 5th ed. (Jersey Shore, PA: Zebrowski Historical Services and Publishing, 1991), 42.

55. William M. Beauchamp, *Civil, Religious and Mourning Councils and Ceremonies of Adoption of the New York Indians* (Albany: University of the State of New York, State Education Department, 1907), 404.

56. Seaver, *Life of Mary Jemison*, 60.

57. Seaver, *Life of Mary Jemison*, 13.

58. Charles Elihu Slocum, *History of the Slocums, Slocumbs, and Slocombs of America: Genealogical and Biographical, Embracing Twelve Generations of the First-Named Family from A.D. 1637 to 1908, with Their Marriages and Descendants in the Female Lines as Far as Ascertained* (Defiance, OH: published by the author, 1908), 194.

59. Slocum, *History*, 199.

60. William Brandon, *New Worlds for Old: Reports from the New World and Their Effect on the Development of Social Thought in Europe, 1500–1800* (Athens, OH: Ohio University Press, 1986), 90, quoted in Jack Weatherford, *Indian Givers* (New York: Three Rivers Press, 2010), 159.

Chapter 7

61. Richard M. Bayles, ed., *History of Windham County, Connecticut* (New York: W.W. Preston, 1889), 50.

62. Barbara Graymont, *The Iroquois in the American Revolution* (Syracuse, NY: Syracuse University Press, 1972). According to Graymont, the decision of the Oneida and Tuscarora to take the side of the Continental forces was strongly due to the influence of a longtime missionary to the Oneida and Tuscarora, Samuel Kirkland. However, each warrior in the Haudenosaunee was still free to decide for himself whether or not fight, and on which side.

63. Allan W. Eckert, *The Wilderness War* (Boston: Little, Brown, 1978), 183.

64. Graymont, *Iroquois in the American Revolution*, 167–68. The Tuscarora Sagwarithra is referred to as a "sachem" by Graymont. There are fifty sachem names, and they are distributed differently among the five original members of the Haudenosaunee. The Tuscarora, who joined the Iroquois Confederacy in the 1700s, originally did not have any sachems who could sit as equals with the rest of the Confederacy (Morgan, *League of the Iroquois*, 98). Currently the Tuscarora have a Council of Chiefs appointed by the clan mothers, in keeping with traditional Haudenosaunee practice, and thirteen chiefs. (See Anthony F.C. Wallace, *Tuscarora: A History* [Albany: State University of New York Press, 2012], 184.)

65. Anthony F.C. Wallace, *The Death and Rebirth of the Seneca* (New York: Vintage Books, 1972), 137.

66. A. Tiffany Norton, *History of Sullivan's Campaign against the Iroquois* (Lima, NY: A. Tiffany Norton, 1879), 22.

67. Eckert, *Wilderness War*, 210.

68. Graymont, *Iroquois in the American Revolution*, 172.

69. Eckert, *Wilderness War*, 222–23.

70. Craft, *History of Bradford County*, 74.

71. Eckert, *Wilderness War*, 217–18.

72. Stephen B. Killian, Esq., from a narrative created for tours of the Wyoming Battle site. Many of these stories, as well as illustrations in the collection of Killian, appear in a book written by George Peck: *Wyoming: Its History, Stirring Incidents, and Romantic Adventures* (New York: Harper & Bros., 1858).

73. Peck, *Wyoming*, 371.

74. Graymont, *Iroquois in the American Revolution*, 174.

75. Wallace, *Death*, 137–38.

76. Wm. Wright, "A Fugitive from the Massacre [Letter to the Editor]," in *The Historical Record: A Quarterly Publication Devoted Principally to the Early History of the Wyoming Valley and Contiguous Territory*, ed. F.C. Johnson (Wilkes-Barre, PA: Press of the Wilkes-Barre Record, 1888), 6.

77. Wallace, *Death*, 138.

78. Amanda Fontenova's description was provided to the author in April 2021.

79. Wallace, *Death*, 138.

80. Graymont, *Iroquois in the American Revolution*, 188.

Chapter 8

81. Norton, *History*, 67.

82. Norton, *History*, 70n.

83. Norton, *History*, 76.

84. Graymont, *Iroquois in the American Revolution*, 208–9. Note that individual braves could make an individual choice to fight for the British or Continental forces, apart from the rest of their tribe, as did the Tuscarora Sagwarithra.

85. The word *castle* was used by the Haudenosaunee to refer to towns.

86. Graymont, *Iroquois in the American Revolution*, 213.

87. Frederick Cook, *Journals of the Military Expedition of Major General John Sullivan against the Six Nations of Indians in 1779* (Westminster, MD: Heritage, 1887), 244. This incident also appears in the diary of Lieutenant William Barton, General Maxwell's New Jersey Brigade; see Cook, *Journals*, 8.

88. Seaver, *Life of Mary Jemison*, 120–21.

89. Killian, narrative.

90. Canby, *American Indian Law*, 68

Chapter 9

91. William Henry Egle, *An Illustrated History of the Commonwealth of Pennsylvania, Civil, Political, and Military, from Its Earliest Settlements to the Present Times* (Harrisburg, PA: De Witt C. Goodrich, 1876), 882–83.

92. Peck, *Wyoming*, 335.

93. Taylor, *SCP 9*, 132.

94. Eberhardt, *Hearts*, 10.
95. Williams T. Blair, *The Michael Shoemaker Book* (Scranton, PA: International Textbook, 1924), 570n. Note: Lydia was a young daughter of Zebulon Marcy.
96. Eberhardt, *Hearts*, 45.

Chapter 10

97. The spelling of Earle varies from Earle to Earll and Earl, probably due to the lack of, or the poor state of, schooling for early settlers of New England, New York and Pennsylvania.
98. Taylor, *SCP 9*, 267.
99. Bayles, *History of Windham*, 40–42.
100. Samuel W. Durant, *History of Kalamazoo County, Michigan, with Illustrations and Biographical Sketches of Prominent Men and Pioneers* (Philadelphia: Everts & Abbott, 1880), 376. Yates County was formed from Ontario County, New York.
101. Lorraine Cook White, ed., *The Barbour Collection of Connecticut Town Vital Records*, vol. 1, *Pomfret Connecticut: Pomfret Vital Statistics*, 145.
102. Walter P. Hinchman, *Pomfret: Through the Years* (Pomfret, Connecticut: Pomfret Historical Society, 2013), 59.
103. Jeptha/Jephthah Earl lived in Wilkes-Barre, Pennsylvania, where he married Bridget Arthur in 1789 at the age of twenty-two. After his marriage, he removed to Seneca, near Geneva, New York (Stafford Canning Cleveland, *History and Directory of Yates County* [Penn Yan, NY: S.C. Cleveland, 1873], 179). Although he was not directly involved, he gave a deposition regarding the kidnapping (Taylor, *SCP 9*, 469n). In New York, Jephthah lived near Solomon at Kashong, Seneca Lake, and next to Daniel in Seneca. It appears from these facts that he was a relative of the family of Joseph, Solomon, Benjamin and Daniel Earl.
104. Taylor, *SCP 9*, 198. It was signed by ten of the fifteen kidnappers ("Benjamin, Daniel and Solomon Earll, Frederick Budd, David Woodward, John Hyde Jr, Ira Manvil, Gideon Dudley, Joseph Dudley, Zebulon Cady") and their relatives.
105. John C. Williams, *The History and Map of Danby, Vermont* (Rutland, VT: McLean & Robbins, 1869), 136; Abby Maria Hemenway, *The Vermont Historical Gazeteer*, vol. 3, *Orleans and Rutland Counties* (Claremont, NH: Claremont Manufacturing, 1877), 620.

106. J. Robert Maguire, "Hand's Cove: Rendezvous of Ethan Allen and the Green Mountain Boys for the Capture of Fort Ticonderoga," *Vermont History* 33, no. 4 (October 1965): 418.

107. James S. Hannum, *The Earl and Arrell Families from Ireland to North America* (Baltimore, MD: Gateway, 2000), 8.

108. Hannum, *Earl and Arrell Families*, 98.

109. Taylor, *SCP 9*, 442.

110. Taylor, *SCP 9*, 490.

111. Taylor, *SCP 9*, 471.

112. A cordwainer made shoes from leather, as opposed to the lower-status cobbler, who was restricted to repairing shoes in Britain.

113. Andi Rierden, "The View from: Dudleytown; A Hamlet That Can't Get Rid of Its Ghosts," *New York Times*, October 29, 1989, Section CN, 12, https://www.nytimes.com/1989/10/29/nyregion/the-view-from-dudleytown-a-hamlet-that-can-t-get-rid-of-its-ghosts.html.

114. Taylor, *SCP 9*, 407.

115. This could also be an uncle and nephew, as the term "Jr." was sometimes applied to related persons of the same name.

116. Taylor, *SCP 9*, 420.

117. Craft, *History of Bradford County*, 273.

118. Taylor, *SCP 9*, 407.

119. "Marker Is Placed on Grave of Revolutionary Soldier," *Scranton Republican* (September 15, 1924): 17.

120. Taylor, *SCP 9*, 408.

121. Taylor, *SCP 9*, 485–86.

Chapter 11

122. Miner, *History*, 429n.

123. Taylor, *SCP 9*, 392.

124. Taylor, *SCP 9*, 409–10.

125. The Abbots were not directly involved in the kidnapping but provided support. Pickering listed five Boys who joined the party after the kidnapping: Noah Phelps, William Carney, Nathan Abbot, Benjamin Abbot and Aaron Kilborn (Taylor, *SCP 9*, 438).

126. Taylor, *SCP 9*, 434–35.

127. Taylor, *SCP 9*, 411–12.

128. Taylor, *SCP 9*, 428, 437.

129. Taylor, *SCP 9*, 434.

130. Taylor, *SCP 9*, 440–41.

131 Taylor, *SCP 9*, 418–20.

132. Taylor, *SCP 9*, 480–81.

133. Taylor, *SCP 9*, 517.

134. Taylor, *SCP 9*, 516.

135. Taylor, *SCP 9*, 435.

136. Moyer, *Wild Yankees*, 154.

137. Fenton, *Great Law*, 627.

Chapter 12

138. Diedrich Willers, *Centennial Historical Sketch of the Town of Fayette, Seneca County, New York* (Geneva, NY: W.F. Humphrey, 1900), 22.

139. George Stillwell Conover, ed., and Lewis Cass Aldrich, comp., *History of Ontario County, NY* (Syracuse, NY: D. Mason, 1893), 18.

140. Taylor, *SCP 9*, 218.

141. Orasmus Turner, *History of the Pioneer Settlement of Phelps and Gorham's Purchase and Morris Reserve* (Rochester, NY: William Alling, 1851), 378–79. In this account, Turner adds, "Horrid and lawless as it may now seem, it was justified by then existing exigencies"; Orasmus Turner, *Pioneer History of the Holland Purchase of Western New York* (Buffalo: Jewett, Thomas; Geo. H. Derby, 1849), 365n; Conover and Aldrich, *History of Ontario County*, 17–18.

142. Turner, *Pioneer History of the Holland Purchase*, 488.

143. Turner, *Pioneer History of the Holland Purchase*, 379; also in Turner, *Phelps and Gorham's Purchase*, 432.

144. Wallace, *Tuscarora*, 79.

145. Stuart D. Scott, Patricia Kay Scott and Paul Mathew Masca, *An Archeological Survey of Artpark and the Lower Landing Lewiston, NY* (Lewiston: Lewiston Historical Society, 1993), 121, cited in Wallace, *Tuscarora*, 81.

BIBLIOGRAPHY

Note: Sources for vital statistics and family histories were found in libraries or online genealogical sites and are not included here unless they were directly quoted in the text or provide an important reference.

Anderson, Robert Charles. *The Great Migration Directory: Immigrants to New England 1620–1640.* Boston: New England Historic Genealogical Society, 2015.

Bayles, Richard M., ed. *History of Windham County, Connecticut.* New York: W.W. Preston, 1889.

Beauchamp, William M. *Civil, Religious and Mourning Councils and Ceremonies of Adoption of the New York Indians.* Albany: University of the State of New York, State Education Department, 1907.

Blair, Williams T. *The Michael Shoemaker Book.* Scranton, PA: International Textbook Press, 1924.

Boyd, Julian P., and Robert J. Taylor, eds. *The Susquehannah Company Papers.* 11 vols. Ithaca, NY: Cornell University Press, 1962–71.

Bradsby, H.C. *History of Bradford County, Pennsylvania, with Biographical Selections.* Chicago: S.B. Nelson, 1891.

———. *History of Luzerne County, Pennsylvania, with Biographical Selections.* Chicago: S.B. Nelson, 1893.

Brubaker, Jack. *Massacre of the Conestogas.* Charleston, SC: The History Press, 2013.

Canby, William C., Jr. *American Indian Law in a Nutshell.* 3rd ed. St. Paul, Minnesota: West Group, 1998.

Clarfield, Gerard H. *Timothy Pickering and the American Republic.* Pittsburg: University of Pittsburg Press, 1980.

Cleveland, Stafford Canning. *History and Directory of Yates County.* Penn Yan, NY: S.C. Cleveland, 1873.

Conover, George Stillwell, ed., and Lewis Cass Aldrich, comp. *History of Ontario County, NY.* Syracuse, NY: D. Mason, 1893.

Converse, Harriet Maxwell (Ya-ie-wa-noh). *Myths and Legends of the New York State Iroquois.* Albany: University of the State of New York, State Education Department, 1908.

Cook, Frederick. *Journals of the Military Expedition of Major General John Sullivan against the Six Nations of Indians in 1779.* Westminster, MD: Heritage, 1887.

Craft, David. *History of Bradford County, Pennsylvania with Illustrations and Biographical Sketches of Some of Its Prominent Men and Pioneers.* Philadelphia: L.H. Everts, 1878.

Doherty, Frank J. *The Settlers of the Beekman Patent, Dutchess County, New York: An Historical and Genealogical Study of All the 18th Century Settlers in the Patent.* Vol. 4. Pleasant Valley, NY: Frank J. Doherty, 1990–2003.

Durant, Samuel W. *History of Kalamazoo County, Michigan, with Illustrations and Biographical Sketches of Prominent Men and Pioneers.* Philadelphia: Everts & Abbott, 1880.

Dye, Kitty. *Maconaquah's Story: The Saga of Frances Slocum.* Inchem Publishing, 1996.

Earle, Pliny. *The Earle Family: Ralph Earle and His Descendants.* Worcester, MA: Charles Hamilton, 1888.

Eberhardt, Mrs. William (Hatsy). *Hearts Nerved to Endure: The Story of Zebulon Marcy, First Settler of Tunkhannock, PA.* Tunkhannock, PA: Bicentennial Committee, Tunkhannock Junior Women's Club, 1976.

Eckert, Allan W. *The Wilderness War.* Boston: Little, Brown and Company, 1978.

Egle, William Henry. *Documents Relating to the Connecticut Settlement of the Wyoming Valley.* Harrisburg: E.K. Meyers, 1893.

———. *An Illustrated History of the Commonwealth of Pennsylvania, Civil, Political, and Military, from Its Earliest Settlements to the Present Times.* Harrisburg, PA: De Witt C. Goodrich, 1876.

———. *Some Pennsylvania Women During the War of the Revolution.* 1898; repr., Baltimore, MD: Clearfield, 1993.

Fenton, William N. *The False Faces of the Iroquois.* Norman: University of Oklahoma Press, 1987.

————. *The Great Law and the Longhouse.* Norman: University of Oklahoma Press, 1998.

Franklin, Benjamin. "A Narrative of the Late Massacres, [30 January? 1764]." In *The Papers of Benjamin Franklin*, vol. 11, *January 1, through December 31, 1764,* edited by Leonard W. Larabee, 42–69. New Haven, CT: Yale University Press, 1967. https://founders.archives.gov/documents/Franklin/01-11-02-0012.

Godcharles, Frederick A. "Pennsylvanians, Past and Present." *New Castle News*, Friday, September 26, 1834, 12.

Graymont, Barbara. *The Iroquois.* New York: Chelsea House, 1988.

————. *The Iroquois in the American Revolution.* Syracuse, NY: Syracuse University Press, 1972.

Hannum, James S. *The Earl and Arrell Families from Ireland to North America.* Baltimore, MD: Gateway, 2000.

Hayden, Horace Edwin, ed. *Proceedings and Collections of the Wyoming County Historical and Genealogical Society for the Year 1901.* Vol. 7. Wilkes-Barre: E.B. Yordy, 1902.

Hemenway, Abby Maria. *The Vermont Historical Gazeteer*, vol. 3, *Orleans and Rutland Counties.* Claremont, NH: Claremont Manufacturing, 1877.

Heverly, Clement Ferdinand. *History and Geography of Bradford County, PA, 1615–1924.* Towanda, PA: Bradford Co. Historical Society, 1926.

Hinchman, Walter P., ed. *Pomfret: Through the Years.* Pomfret, CT: Pomfret Historical Society, 2013.

Hollister, Horace. *History of Lackawanna Valley.* 5th ed. Philadelphia: J.B. Lippincott Company, 1885.

Jacobus, Donald Lines. "Churchmen of 1738, Under Rev. Jonathan Arnold of West Haven, Connecticut." *American Genealogist* 34 (April 1958): 54–64.

Jenness, Diamond. *The Indians of Canada.* 7th ed. Toronto: University of Toronto Press, 1977.

Johnson, F.C., ed. *The Historical Record: A Quarterly Publication Devoted Principally to the Early History of the Wyoming Valley and Contiguous Territory.* Vol. 2. Wilkes-Barre, PA: Press of the Wilkes-Barre Record, 1888.

Kinner, Oliver Smith. "An Interesting Narrative of Early Settlements by Indians and Whites in These Parts." *Lest We Forget* 12, no. 1 (September 15, 1992): 32.

Kuhl, Jackson. "The Incredibly Convoluted History of Westmoreland County, Connecticut." *Journal of the American Revolution* (October 29, 2014). https://allthingsliberty.com/author/jackson-kuhl/.

Larmenter, Jon. "The Meaning of *Kaswentha* and the Two-Row Wampum Belt in Haudenosaunee (Iroquois) History: Can Indigenous Oral Tradition Be Reconciled with the Documentary Record?" *Journal of Early American History* 3 (2013): 82–109: http://honorthetworow.org/wp-content/uploads/2012/01/The-Meaning-of-Kaswentha-and-the-Two-Row.pdf.

Larned, Ellen Douglas. *History of Windham County, Connecticut.* Vol. 1. Worcester, MA: published by the author, 1874.

Maguire, J. Robert. "Hand's Cove: Rendezvous of Ethan Allen and the Green Mountain Boys for the Capture of Fort Ticonderoga." *Vermont History* 33, no. 4 (October 1965): 417–37.

"Marker Is Placed on Grave of Revolutionary Soldier." *Scranton Republican*, September 15, 1924, 17.

McCracken, George E. "The Connecticut Pennsylvanians." *American Genealogist* 55, no. 2 (April 1979): 72–82.

Miller, Spencer. "Earle Family of Bishop's Stortford, Co., Herts, England." *NY Genealogical and Biological Record* 57, no. 4 (1936): 390–93.

Milliken, Charles F. *A History of Ontario County, New York and Its People.* New York: Lewis Historical Publishing, 1911.

Miner, Charles. *History of Wyoming in a Series of Letters from Charles Miner to His Son William Penn Miner, Esq.* Philadelphia: J. Crissy, 1845.

Monroe, Joel Henry. *A Century and a Quarter of History of Geneva from 1787 to 1912.* Geneva, NY: W.F. Humphrey, 1912.

Morgan, Lewis Henry. *League of the Iroquois.* New York: Corinth Books, 1962.

Moyer, Paul B. *Wild Yankees: The Struggle for Independence along Pennsylvania's Revolutionary Frontier.* Ithaca, NY: Cornell University Press, 2007.

Munger, Donna B. *Connecticut's Pennsylvania "Colony" 1754–1810: Susquehanna Proprietors, Settlers, and Claimants.* Vol. 1. Westminster, MD: Heritage Books, 2007.

Munsell, W.W. *History of Luzerne, Lackawanna and Wyoming Counties, PA with Illustrations and Biographical Sketches of Some of Their Prominent Men and Pioneers.* New York: W.W. Munsell, 1880.

Nabokov, Peter, ed. *Native American Testimony: A Chronicle of Indian-White Relations from Prophecy to the Present 1492–1992.* New York: Penguin, 1991.

Norton, A. Tiffany. *History of Sullivan's Campaign against the Iroquois.* Lima, NY: A. Tiffany Norton, 1879.

Oscar, Jewell Harvey, and Ernest Gray Smith. *A History of Wilkes-Barre, Luzerne County, Pennsylvania, from Its First Beginnings to the Present Time…* Wilkes-Barre, PA: Lodge of Masons, 1930.

Parker, Arthur C. *Parker on the Iroquois.* Syracuse, NY: Syracuse University Press, 1968.

Peck, George. *Wyoming: Its History, Stirring Incidents, and Romantic Adventures.* New York: Harper & Bros., 1858.

Pennsylvania Historical and Museum Commission. "1681–1776: The Quaker Province." http://www.phmc.state.pa.us/portal/communities/pa-history/1681-1776.html.

Pickering, Timothy. *Timothy Pickering Papers.* Massachusetts Historical Society. https://www.masshist.org/collection-guides/view/fa0256.

Pomfret, John E. "The First Purchasers of Pennsylvania 1681–1700." *Pennsylvania Magazine of History and Biography* 80, no. 1 (1956): 137–63.

Prucha, Francis Paul, ed. *Documents of United States Indian Policy.* 2nd ed. Lincoln: University of Nebraska Press, 1990.

Rierden, Andi. "The View from: Dudleytown, A Hamlet That Can't Get Rid of Its Ghosts." *New York Times*, October 29, 1989, Section CN, 12. https://www.nytimes.com/1989/10/29/nyregion/the-view-from-dudleytown-a-hamlet-that-can-t-get-rid-of-its-ghosts.html.

Ross, Rupert. *Dancing with a Ghost.* Toronto: Penguin Canada, 2006.

Schaaf, Gregory. *Wampum Belts and Peace Trees.* Golden, CO: Fulcrum, 1990.

Scott, Stuart D., Patricia Kay Scott, and Paul Mathew Masca. *An Archeological Survey of Artpark and the Lower Landing Lewiston, NY.* Lewison: Lewiston Historical Society, 1993. In *Tuscarora: A History*, Anthony F.C. Wallace, 81. Albany: State University of New York Press, 2012.

Seaver, James E. *The Life of Mary Jemison.* 5th ed. Jersey Shore, PA: Zebrowski Historical Services and Publishing, 1991.

Slocum, Charles Elihu. *History of the Slocums, Slocumbs, and Slocombs of America: Genealogical and Biographical, Embracing Twelve Generations of the First-Named Family from A.D. 1637 to 1908, with Their Marriages and Descendants in the Female Lines As Far As Ascertained.* Vol. 2. Defiance, OH: published by the author, 1908.

Speck, Frank Gouldsmith. *The Iroquois: A Study in Cultural Evolution.* 2nd ed. Bloomfield Hills, MI: Clanbrook Institute of Science, 1982.

Start, Bruce B. "The Charter of 1662." ConnecticutHistory.org. July 18, 2019. https://connecticuthistory.org/the-charter-of-1662/.

Storke, Elliot G. *History of Cayuga County, New York.* Syracuse, NY: D. Mason, 1879.

Susquehanna Company Records, Liber I. Records of deeds kept by John and Billa Franklin, 1786–1796.

Tehanetorens (Ray Fadden). *Wampum Belts of the Iroquois.* Summertown, TN: Book Publishing Company, 1999.

Turner, Orasmus. *History of the Pioneer Settlement of Phelps and Gorham's Purchase and Morris Reserve.* Rochester: William Alling, 1851.

————. *Pioneer History of the Holland Purchase of Western New York.* Buffalo: Jewett, Thomas; Geo. H. Derby, 1849.

Wallace, Anthony F.C. *The Death and Rebirth of the Seneca.* New York: Vintage Books, 1972.

————. *Tuscarora: A History.* Albany: State University of New York Press, 2012.

Weatherford, Jack. *Indian Givers: How Native Americans Transformed the World.* New York: Three Rivers, 2010.

White, Lorraine Cook, ed. *The Barbour Collection of Connecticut Town Vital Records*, vol. 1, *Pomfret, Connecticut: Pomfret Vital Statistics.*

Willers, Diedrich. *Centennial Historical Sketch of the Town of Fayette, Seneca County, New York.* Geneva, NY: Press of W.F. Humphrey, 1900.

Williams, John C. *The History and Map of Danby, Vermont.* Rutland, VT: McLean & Robbins, 1869.

Williamson, James R., and Linda A. Fossler, *The Susquehanna Frontier: Northeastern Pennsylvania during the Revolutionary Years.* Wilkes-Barre, PA: Wilkes University Press, 1997.

Woodward, Walter W. "From the State Historian: The Map That Wasn't a Map." ConnecticutHistory.org. January 25, 2013. https://connecticuthistory.org/from-the-state-historian-the-map-that-wasnt-a-map/.

Wright, William. "A Fugitive from the Massacre [Letter to the Editor]." In *The Historical Record: A Quarterly Publication Devoted Principally to the Early History of the Wyoming Valley and Contiguous Territory*, vol. 2, edited by F. C. Johnson, 6. Wilkes-Barre, PA: Press of the Wilkes-Barre Record, 1888.

INDEX

ABOUT THE AUTHOR

Kathleen A. Earle is a native New Yorker whose ancestral roots go back to Pennsylvania. She is an author, artist, former professor and former director of research at the National Indian Child Welfare Association in Portland, Oregon. She attended Cornell University and the Rockefeller College of the State University of New York at Albany, where she received a PhD in 1996. She has written and illustrated several award-winning children's books, a book of essays and many peer-reviewed articles in the areas of mental health and child abuse. She lives in Maine with her husband, Stan Fox.

Visit us at
www.historypress.com